THE ONLY

WOMAN

IN THE ROOM

KNOWLEDGE AND INSPIRATION FROM
20 WOMEN REAL ESTATE INVESTORS

COMPILED BY

ASHLEY L. WILSON

www.TheRealEstateInvestHER.com

THE ONLY WOMAN IN THE ROOM:

Knowledge and Inspiration from 20 Successful Women Real Estate Investors

Compiled by Ashley L. Wilson

Co-authored by:

Corinn Altomare, Brittany Arnason, April Crossley, Leka V. Devatha, Melanie Dupuis, Liz Faircloth, Kathy Fettke, Maria Friström, Andresa Guidelli, Anna Kelley, Gertrude Mageza, Serena Norris, Deborah Nye, Patricia L. Red Hawk, MD, Rebecca L. Rynkiewicz, Palak Shah, Rebecca Shea, Rachel Street, Ashley L. Wilson, Grace Yarber

Dedication

This book is dedicated to the trailblazers who came before us, the ones who walk alongside us, and the ones who have yet to come.

Testimonials

"*The Only Woman in the Room* is a book that is long overdue. Real estate investing offers unparalleled opportunities for wealth creation and personal fulfillment regardless of gender. The amazing women profiled in this book prove that to be true. Kudos to Ashley Wilson for compiling these inspirational stories and sage words of advice from 20 of the best in the business. I benefited from reading this book and I know many others will too."

-Brian Murray
Author, Crushing It in Apartments and Commercial Real Estate

"*The Only Woman in the Room* is not just a great book, it's a necessary one. In today's world, achieving financial prosperity is not guaranteed to anyone, and even more so for women. This book tells women what they need to know, and tells it in the voice of many generous other women who want to help their community achieve their goals. The book also doesn't just address money, because that's not what success is. It gives women the path to success in their marriage, families, business, personal discovery, and communities. This is a must-read for any woman looking to lead a vibrant and well-rounded life!"

-Matt Faircloth
Co-Founder of The DeRosa Group and Author of Bigger Pocket's Amazon Best Seller Raising Private Capital

"Throughout my career there were multiple occasions where I have stood as the only woman in the room. This powerful book is a must read and I only wish it had been available early on in my career!"

-Barbara Corcoran
Founder of The Corcoran Group

"This book is a long awaited big step forward in the fight to make the incredible wealth building power of the male dominated real estate investing industry more accessible to women everywhere."

-Scott Trench
CEO, BiggerPockets.com

"Commercial real estate has been traditionally hard for women to break into due to a lack of role models. Well, this book provides 20 role models who are honest, daring and have overcome numerous obstacles to achieve success in the industry. Each and every story helps to inspire and also to make a career investing in real estate accessible to all. I wish there was a resource like this when I first got into commercial real estate over 25 years ago ... as then I might not have been the only woman in the room."

-Diane Danielson
COO, SVN International Corp.

"Someone wise once said, if you want to see far, stand on the shoulders of giants. But I'll add this: if you want to go far in business, stand on the shoulders of many giants. Because the truth is: hearing different perspectives and stories and lessons from multiple people can help you maximize your learning while also helping you avoid costly mistakes. That's exactly what The Only Women in the Room is - a way for you to stand on the shoulders of almost two-dozen highly successful real estate investors - so you can go far! It comes jam-packed with lessons that are highly encouraging for new investors and immensely helpful for those with more experience. Although directed towards women, men can definitely learn a thing or two here... I know I did!"

-Brandon Turner
Host of The BiggerPockets Podcast

"Wow! A truly inspiring collaboration by an impressive group of women beautifully balancing their roles as investors, experts, daughters, wives, and moms. The authors' raw, real, often vulnerable accounts of their successes and failures, their challenges and celebrations, all share a common thread: an unwavering desire to be the very best version of themselves, building a life on their own terms, and motivating others to take that leap of faith to achieve fulfillment and freedom in all its forms."

-Carol J Scott
Best-Selling Author, The Book on Negotiating Real Estate; Owner, Scott Silver Staging & Scott Silver Concierge Realty; Co-Host, The BiggerPockets Business Podcast

"As a fellow female investor I know first hand what it's like to push past boundaries both in business and at home. No matter what level of investor you are there comes a time when you need motivation and inspiration. In the pages you are about to read these women provide just that. You will be shown a glimpse into the real lives of these women and how they continue to grow, learn, and teach. Each piece of advice will leave you as a better investor and person."

-Ashley Kehr
Buy and Hold Investor and Co-Host of BiggerPockets
Real Estate Rookie Podcast

"In any male dominated industry, it takes a group of truly formidable and talented women to break down barriers and provide opportunity to all the women who follow. In the real estate investing world, this is that group of women. I am honored to call them colleagues and friends. In this book, these women lay bare their struggles, their failures, and ultimately, their success not only as investors, but as pioneers."

-J Scott
Entrepreneur, Best-Selling Author, Investor and Co-Host of The Bigger-Pockets Business Podcast

"It's not often that I encounter a book featuring so many of the best investors I know. Investors from all walks of life, who have taken on all sorts of obstacles. Not only does *The Only Women in the Room* cover strategies employed by these investors but just as importantly it covers the stories behind them. Success leaves clues, and this is a book full of them."

-Dave Van Horn
President & CEO, PPR Note Co.

Contents

Introduction
by Ashley L. Wilson

A brilliant 80-year-old woman once said to me, "I decided to switch careers from an astrophysicist to a real estate investor when I realized that it was the only profession where my gender did not affect my earning potential." I do not know what I was more impressed with: that this was the first woman I had met who had been investing for over 50 years, or that five decades ago she had already identified the power of investing in real estate that I only discovered ten years prior.

As a woman who has invested in real estate over the past decade, I have met several people, both women and men, who have inspired me and shaped me into the investor I am today. While I wish my role models were more balanced between genders, I know without question they are overwhelmingly men. Like my realization of real estate investing, my realization of how this field is dominated by men did not come to my attention right away.

In 2018, I attended a multi-day real estate investing conference. During this conference, Liz Faircloth and Andresa Guidelli, Co-Founders of The Real Estate InvestHER®, invited all the women in attendance to lunch. It took only two tables squeezed together to accommodate all 16 of us. In other words, less than 4% of the total attendees at the conference were women.

At this lunch I finally became cognizant of the lack of women in the room. You know the saying, "it came over me like a wave?" This was that moment. Flashbacks of several other real estate events I attended whizzed through my mind, and all these memories had an overwhelming number of men attendees and presenters. As a woman myself, how had I become so numb to this obvious trend it took me eight years within real estate investing to see it?

I promised myself, at that very moment, that I would write a book around the concept of being the only woman in the room. I wanted this book to highlight what I had failed to see, spotlight badass real estate women investors, provide knowledge, inspiration and most importantly give examples of female real estate investing role models that could inspire anyone (woman or man).

Over the next year, I identified 19 incredible women who have inspired, educated and motivated me. While they differ on various levels, they have one thing in common; they are all incredibly generous with their time, knowledge and support. A quintessential example of this is evident in each chapter.

Another similarity is that most of us shared the lack of female real estate investor role models. As the mother of two daughters, I wanted to change this. All these women have characteristics I want my daughters to have: drive, intelligence, grit, passion and generosity.

Having a seat at the table is a phrase that has often been used to capture the challenge women face when being included with people of power. It is not lost on me the irony that my realization of the lack of women in real estate investing came while sitting at a table full of women. To women everywhere, I hope this book serves as an invite that you are welcome to join our figurative table. You are no longer the only woman in the room.

The Key to Financial Freedom
by Ashley L. Wilson

We cannot all succeed when half of us are held back.
–Malala Yousafzai

At a very early age, I knew I wanted to live my life on my terms. I remember thinking, I want the freedom to be there for my kids, just like my parents were, and still are, for me and my brother. Despite both my parents working full-time, they each had jobs that allowed them flexibility. My mom was fortunate enough to work for a company that allowed her to adjust her schedule as needed, and my dad was self-employed, allowing him to make his own hours. Assessing both of my parents' situations, I decided being an entrepreneur was the surest way to guarantee my goal of financial freedom.

Over the next two decades, I pursued several ventures ultimately landing in real estate. During this journey I knew everything I was doing was leading me to my goal. I did not realize how much I would learn about how many other women were struggling to achieve this very same goal.

Setting the Scene

Throughout my life, I have been surrounded by men more often than women. My brother's teammates from the various teams he played on often came over to our house, I attended a previously all-boys school where the boys outnumbered the girls three to one, and in college, I lived in a house with 14 other boys. I know, crazy, right? However, I was more comfortable being around boys than I was with girls. I liked the way they thought, I liked the ease at which they got over conflict, and I liked the opportunities that always seemed to come their way. Honestly, it was simply easier to be around boys than girls.

For the past ten years, I have immersed myself into real estate and while I did not initially realize it, I found myself once again primarily surrounded by men. Often, and still, to this very day, I find myself at meetings, tables and events where men dominate the room (both from a presentation standpoint and a physical one).

Ah-Ha Moment

In the spring of 2018, I attended a multi-day real estate conference where I, along with every other woman in attendance, was asked to sit together during one of the lunches. This request was initiated by Liz Faircloth and Andresa Guidelli, the Co-Founders of The Real Estate InvestHer©. There were over 450 people at that conference, and less than 20 women sat at the table (less than 5% of the attendees). While everyone was getting to know each other, I was in awe by our squeezing only two tables together to fit us all. It was the first time I realized how few women were in attendance.

From that very moment, literally at the table, I promised myself I would write a book titled, *The Only Woman in the Room*. My goal was to bring more women to this table. I did not know how I would do it, *yet*, but my mind was intrigued, and if you know me, you already know that once I say I will do something, I am one determined BadAsh!

Eyes Wide Open

Have you ever noticed that when you like a specific car, it seems to drive past you more frequently? That same concept happened to me as I realized how often I would attend a real estate meet-up and be one of the few, if not the only, women in the room. I also noticed how men dominated as speakers. Even today, I still see conferences that have only male speakers! As a very quizzical person, I pondered the next logical question, *Why*. Why are there little to no women in attendance? Why are there so few women speakers?

My list of questions expanded further, when a few months after that infamous eye-opening conference, I tried to raise money for an apartment investment opportunity. Woman after woman I spoke to said, "Not interested," or "I have to speak to my spouse first," then ultimately replying with "Not interested." Fortunately, I had a significantly better success rate when it came to speaking to men. This situation added a new *Why* to my ever-growing list of questions; *Why were women not investing in real estate?*

In my quest to find the answers to each question, I kept landing on one direct link - the gender divide. The divide is both intentional and unintentional and is witnessed on multiple fronts with the most common one people think of as being the wage gap. Unfortunately, it starts way before you enter the workforce; you are born into the divide.

Life Expectancy

It is a running, albeit sick, joke my husband and I have when we speak about what will happen when one of us dies. My husband's Achilles heel is locating items and mine is anything to do with technology. The truth is although my husband is younger than I am, I will most likely outlive him. According to the World Health Organization, women live on average between six to eight years longer than men (https://www.who.int/gho/women_and_health/mortality/situation_trends_life_expectancy/en/). If this comes to fruition, while there is no doubt in my mind I will still struggle with technology, I will have the ability to sustain a living and surviving off the earnings of former years will be of utmost importance.

Today, the Bureau of Labor Statistics reports the cost of living at almost $4,000 a month for an elderly person. Without being too grim, I would need to have an additional $288,000 to $384,000 saved up to just cover the cost of my living expenses if my husband passes away before me, assuming we are the same age.

Wage Gap

The most common example people reference when speaking on the gender divide is the wage gap. Women are literally shortchanged when it comes to equitable compensation which greatly affects their ability to achieve financial freedom. Specifically, women currently make $.79 to every $1.00 that a man makes, and this gap is wider with women who are disabled and women of color (https://money.com/investing-finance-gender-gap-pay-inequality/).

Reluctance to Invest

Unfortunately, these are not the only two factors causing the financial divide between men and women. There is a compounding element, causing the divide to grow exponentially. What is it? Women are 40% less likely to invest than men (https://www.nbcnews.com/better/business/why-women-invest-40-percent-less-men-how-we-can-ncna912956). If you are not in awe of that statistic, let me break it down for you.

Some argue women are less likely to invest because they have less to invest with. The implications of not having as much to invest with, coupled with women being less likely to invest at an earlier age, magnifies the problem to the tune of over one million dollars during a 35-year career, as reported by Ellevest and Money Magazine in 2018 (https://money.com/investing-finance-gender-gap-pay-inequality/).

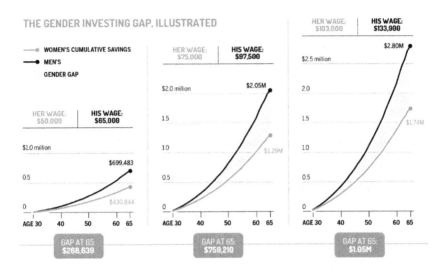

We now know the problem and its profound effects so the next logical step is to ask, how did we get here, so we can identify swift solutions to create change.

Education and Career Paths

Cue the go back in time music. For hundreds of generations, women stayed at home raising children. Although this has changed in the last hundred years, opportunities offered to women are limited to the exposure of knowledge they received. In recent years women were primarily educated for non-STEM (science, technology, engineering and mathematics) careers. While careers in any of those four fields can be very lucrative, mathematical comprehension is essential to succeed in life! Mathematics is the foundation of finance, and finance is the foundation of investing. Ironically, when you build a house, you start with a foundation (mathematics), then you can erect walls (finance) and finally, you finish the structure by enclosing it with a roof (investing). A roof cannot do its job unless it is sitting on level walls and resting on a stable foundation. Like a house, one will not invest, nor succeed at investing, if they do not have a solid comprehension of finance, built on a solid foundation of mathematics. It is no surprise that women have historically been risk-averse for investing, as most women were not exposed to the building blocks of mathematics and finance comprehension that leads one to see the power of investing.

Interestingly, when women do invest, they outperform men as measured by returns (https://www.ft.com/content/f3835072-66a6-11e9-9adc-98bf1d35a056). Not surprisingly, when knowledge meets opportunity, success can be achieved. As women are encouraged to pursue education and careers in STEM, the gap in knowledge will decrease, opening opportunities for a greater comprehension of finance and investing.

Why Does This Matter?

The gender divide as it relates to reluctance to invest, education, wage gap and life expectancy should be a concern for all, regardless of whether you are a woman. As a man, if you have a wife, mother, sister, daughter, aunt, cousin, female friend, etc., you are indirectly affected. Financial strain often becomes the responsibility of supporting family members. In January 2020, the American Association of Retired Persons found that 32 percent of midlife adults have provided some form of financial support within the past year to their parents. Looking into the future, 42 percent believe they will provide financial support in the future. This is a problem for everyone, regardless of gender.

Where to Start

"Knowledge is Power" is a well-known saying and applies perfectly in this situation. Educate yourself on the power of investing. Educate yourself on different investing opportunities. Some people often use a commission-based financial planner to perform this activity, but be mindful of how they are compensated. Commission-based financial planners are only compensated if you invest in certain investments. However, those investments might not be well-suited for your individual financial situation. Consulting a fee-based financial advisor or a Certified Public Accountant (CPA) who knows your financial situation intimately and, therefore, can help you achieve your goals without a biased approach will give you the soundest advice. If you are reading this saying, "I do not know a fee-based financial advisor," or "My CPA does not provide this service," find one and switch!

Support each other through helping all genders see the divide; we cannot all come together to fix a problem that only half of us can see. If you are in the position of power, meaning you already understand the power of investing, educate others. Remind them that wealth is not a prerequisite to investing, but that investing is a prerequisite for wealth.

Ultimately, the path to financial freedom does come through money. Money is often synonymous with power but allowing money to have power over you can turn it into handcuffs. You are tied to it. These handcuffs come in various metals (nickel, silver, bronze, gold and platinum) depending on the dependency one has to money. People who earn seven figures can be tied to money as much as someone making a low five-figure salary. For example, a person could make $40,000 a year with living expenses of only $20,000 and have greater financial freedom than the platinum cuffed executive making one million dollars a year, whose annual expenses total one million five hundred thousand dollars.

No matter the income level, these people are a slave to the power that money provides. Money can take another form, a superpower. This superpower is the key that unlocks those handcuffs, providing financial freedom at all levels.

Initially, I thought the path to financial freedom was simply becoming an entrepreneur. An entrepreneur owns their ideas, sets their own hours and does not have to answer to superiors, which allows for infinite earning potential. While that may be the means in which freedom is achieved, that is not the how. I discovered the how by leveraging the superpower money has. I have identified ways money works for me and not the other way around. Specifically, I buy cash flowing assets that pay me while I sleep. While my money is hard at work for me, I am achieving the ultimate goal I set out to achieve, spending time with my kids. Now that I have given you the key, the question is, will you unlock the superpower?

Ashley L. Wilson

Ashley Wilson, also known as "BadAsh Investor," started investing in real estate in 2010, and is the Co-Founder of HouseItLook LLC and Bar Down Investments, LLC. Previously, Ashley worked for Sanofi-Aventis, Wyeth (Pfizer), and GlaxoSmithKline where she achieved the role of Director of Global Project Management within the department Vaccine Clinical Research and Development. During this period, she learned effective skills to manage from afar. Ashley has since applied these skills to real estate. Specifically, she co-founded HouseItLook, a house flipping company in the suburbs of Philadelphia, with her father Tom while living in Europe. Ashley also co-founded Bar Down Investments with her husband Kyle, specializing in owning and operating large multifamily properties throughout the United States. Besides her two companies, she provides consulting services to other multifamily owners, coaches other real estate investors and speaks regularly at conferences across the country. When Ashley is not working on her businesses, she enjoys spending time with her family, including her husband and their two daughters and competing with her horse, Wow!.

You can learn more about Ashley at www.BadAshInvestor.com, or on Instagram @BadAshInvestor

Overcoming Adversity and Setbacks to Build a Multi-Million Dollar Portfolio
by Anna Kelley

Character cannot be developed in ease and quiet. Only through experiences of trial and suffering can the soul be strengthened, vision cleared, ambition inspired, and success achieved.
–Helen Keller

In America, women are 35% more likely than men to be poor. In fact, 70% of the nation's poor are women and children. According to the Urban Institute, only 16% of persistently poor children, who spend half their childhood in poverty, are consistently working or in school in their late 20s. Worse yet, 64% do not have improved stable employment by the time they reach their 30s. By the grace of God, I beat the statistics and escaped persistent poverty. And by the grace of God, through much adversity and many setbacks, I have built a net worth in the top 3% of U.S. households today.

Overcoming the Odds: A Powerful Motivation

One of my earliest memories was moving in the middle of the night at age 6, to escape another night of abuse at the hands of my stepfather.

My pregnant mom, sister, and I moved in with my grandparents until she found a job as a leasing agent in a Section 8 apartment complex in Texas. She also waitressed at night to support us. The rest of our needs were covered by food stamps. My mom could not afford a babysitter, so at nine years old, I began watching my siblings overnight. My mother loved us and did the best she could to give us a normal life, but life for a single mom and her children in poverty was hard.

My mom eventually remarried and had more children, and the cycle of alcohol, drugs and abuse continued. We found ourselves in battered women shelters and on the couches of family members multiple times. My only escapes were the large tree in our courtyard, school and music.

I saw that my schoolmates' families who made better choices had greater success, wealth and happiness. To escape the projects, I knew I had to spend my time and effort, becoming the best at every opportunity I was given. So, I practiced my flute and studied for hours, hoping for scholarships. I also knew that if I wanted something, I had to make my own money to buy it. I sold candy, made things, and went door to door to sell them, and got a job in eighth grade to buy a nicer flute. While I tried to fit in, kids whispered about how poor I was. It pierced my heart with shame and shook my confidence. I could only hope that one day I would escape the kind of life I was given for one more like theirs.

At 15, I called my father and stepmother and asked to move in with them. Leaving my mother and siblings was one of the hardest decisions I have ever made. I feared that if I did not stay to protect them, they would end up dead. Yet, I also knew I had to get out and think about my own future. I was filled with guilt, sadness and fear for leaving them behind, yet I was relieved and hopeful for the future. I longed for a better life and had a profound sense that God would lead me to greater things.

Making the Most of Every Opportunity

My new home life was very different. Life with two working parents, without drugs and alcohol, and centered around our faith in Christ was much more peaceful. My stepmom reinforced the importance of getting a college education so I could take care of myself and never have to worry about relying on a man to take care of me financially. This realization gave me the determination to relentlessly pursue success and independence with all I had.

I graduated high school early. I also graduated college early, while working full-time and winning two employee of the year awards. I was then hired at Bank of America and won the award for top financial relationship manager in Texas during my first year, despite being underqualified. Finally, I landed a lucrative job at AIG. I credit much of my success to realizing we can only achieve extraordinary success when we push through every hurdle, fear and excuse and go for what we want, even when it seems unlikely, if not impossible.

As life went on, I thought I had made it. I escaped poverty, married a doctor and had a comfortable life and career. I was determined to continue up the corporate ladder until I had my first child. I knew the moment I first held him that I wanted to pause my career and stay home with my baby. But my husband had a $120,000 college loan, and there was no way for us to live on one income. It broke my heart to put my baby in daycare, and as a latchkey child myself, I did not want to be an absent mom.

Getting Creative and Stepping into the Unknown

Not inclined to give up on a solution, I tried real estate investing. HGTV convinced us flipping houses would be easy and a quick way to replace my income. They lied! We flipped our first house, made many rookie mistakes, and ultimately lost $10,000 on the project. By the time it sold, my husband had also lost his job. With two mortgages, a school loan and a car payment, we were barely making it. I was deflated and depressed.

We had another baby and I was still grieving not being able to stay home with my children. We were convinced that having my husband start his own practice was the only solution. So, we sold our house and moved across the country to start his business. The four of us moved in with my in-laws and we bought our first rental property in 2007. It had an office on the first floor for my husband's business and 3 apartments, which would help cover the mortgage. A year later, we bought and moved into a 4-plex. I just knew my husband's practice would take off, we could buy more small apartment buildings, and I would be home with my babies in no time.

Facing Devastating Setbacks

We never could have imagined that the US would experience one of the worst financial crises in history just a few months later at the end of 2008. AIG almost collapsed, and my job was at risk. I also lost most of the value of my 401(k), which was my only savings. I quickly borrowed what little I had left and used it as a down payment on another 4-unit apartment building. We were hundreds of thousands of dollars in debt, out of money and banks were unwilling to finance more rental properties. Healthcare changes strained my husband's practice and the real estate coach I hired turned out to be a fraud.

My dreams of being a stay-at-home mom were shattered! Having done everything I knew possible to achieve financial stability, nothing went as planned. I was working 80 hours a week between my job, our rentals and my husband's practice. Now raising four children, I was at a crossroads. I knew creating more passive income through real estate was the way forward, but we had to find a way to buy more properties without money and bank financing.

Relentlessly Pursuing My Dreams

In 2014, I developed a five-year plan to buy enough small apartment buildings to allow me to retire. I started structuring deals creatively through seller financing and partnerships and bought distressed properties with upside. We bought ugly properties no one else wanted. My husband and I both worked nearly every day, over our lunch breaks, after work, on weekends and late into the night after our kids went to bed. I handled the acquisition, financing, business plans, contractors and budget. He handled the maintenance and construction.

While we made a great team and had complementary competencies, years of sleepless nights and stress took a toll on us. We also had two large apartment-related disasters in a couple of months' time which exceeded our insurance coverage and set us back financially. My husband wanted me to quit buying more properties, especially ones that required his sweat equity. Both his practice and my job were still far from stable, and my dream to be home with my children was far greater than any pain I was experiencing.

We were so close to having enough cash flow from our rental properties to allow me to retire. If we just pushed through a little longer, we could pivot from doing most of the work ourselves and self-managing to hiring others to do it for us. Thankfully, my husband trusted me enough to continue the journey. We kept buying properties for our own portfolio, and eventually, I purchased larger apartment buildings with partners.

Reaping the Harvest

All the hard work finally paid off! We purchased, renovated and rented enough rental property to replace my 6-figure income, and I retired from AIG at 44. Even more incredibly, we went from a large negative net worth in 2007 to a multimillion-dollar net worth in 2019. I now have active ownership in over $60M of multifamily apartments and have invested in another 2000 doors passively. My journey to financial freedom was achieved through blood, sweat and tears. I am so grateful that I determined to relentlessly pursue this dream, regardless of how long it took!

With my children now in school, my dream of being a stay-at-home mom was not realized the way I envisioned. But I have learned to weather the storms of life with strength, determination, faith and love. I am now enjoying spending a lot more quality time with my children! I have also discovered that time has a way of revealing a greater purpose through our pains, hurdles, failures and setbacks. The bumpy parts of the journey build character, wisdom and strength, which only come through experience. Ultimately, who we are becoming is what leads to our success!

Advice for Women Not Afraid to Venture Out into the Unknown!

As you pursue your own dreams, here are a few pieces of advice that have been instrumental in my own path to success. Wherever your dreams are leading you, do not be afraid to venture into the unknown. I wish you success and joy along the journey!

Envision your dream life. Do not limit your dreams due to lack of resources, skills, money, network or other excuses that make achieving success seemingly improbable.

Create your dream life by design. You must have a purpose greater than the pain you will experience on the journey! Write down your vision and a statement on why your dreams are worth pursuing. Read them daily and do something every day towards making your vision a reality.

Muster up the determination and grit to relentlessly pursue your dreams, come hell or high water! Achievement is lumpy and hard things in life can derail you. When the horse bucks you off and you fall out of the saddle, pull up your big girl panties and get back on!

Choose faith when you feel despair! Believe that every challenge will make you stronger and wiser. Believe that it will be ok. Pray for God to strengthen and guide you. Feelings come and go, but the mindset is a choice!

Believe that you have what it takes to solve every problem. Get in the habit of asking yourself, "How can I?" Brainstorm multiple ways to solve every problem and keep brainstorming and testing solutions until you figure out the way forward.

Develop a support system! Get real and vulnerable. None of us have it all figured out. Be humble enough to ask your peers and mentors for guidance and encouragement. If you do not have support, consider joining a mastermind.

Master your time and money, or time and money will master you! Time-block your day and only work on what you can fit in your schedule.

Include time for taking care of yourself and those you love the most. Learn to budget, save, pay off debt and most importantly, to expand your means.

Give yourself grace! Celebrate small wins. They will keep you motivated. Make time for you, because you are important! Forgive yourself when you struggle and make mistakes. You are an amazing, strong woman, but you are not the mythical Wonder Woman. She does not juggle nearly the number of lassos we do!

Anna Kelley

Anna Kelley is the founding partner of Zenith Capital Group, Greater Purpose Capital and <u>ReiMom</u>, LLC. As a former Financial Relationship Manager for a private bank and having developed variable insurance products for high net worth individuals, Anna developed a keen understanding of both traditional and non-traditional investments. She discovered the power of real estate investing, and has since purchased, renovated and rented millions of dollars in rental real estate - all while working full-time and raising four children. She has active ownership in and manages a rental portfolio valued over $60 Million and has invested in over 2000 units. Anna actively seeks the best multi-family investment opportunities for her partners and investors. She is a sought-after speaker and enjoys helping others to overcome fears, increase knowledge and minimize risks in real estate. She is also an Amazon #1 bestselling author.

Dreaming Bigger and Giving Back

Anna is now dreaming of greater things: for herself, her family, and others. She is teaching and inspiring other women to create financial stability and real estate wealth that lasts and has become a sought-after speaker at real estate events across the country. She also started a syndication company focused on sourcing and operating multifamily properties to create strong returns for herself, her partners and her investors. She is proud to be one of the few successful women in the multifamily space today.

She has co-founded Kingdom Minded Investors, a faith-based organization investing in apartments like the one she grew up in, not only for financial returns, but more importantly, for eternal returns in the lives of the people in her communities. She feels blessed to be able to encourage little girls and single moms, that with financial education, determination, faith and hope, they can escape poverty and pursue their own dreams!

Life by Design
by Grace Yarber

Never lose yourself in a relationship. Love your partner fiercely, but always follow your own unique dreams and desires. Be true to you.
–Mama Zara

One of my biggest role models is my mother. She raised two kids, on her own, back in Soviet-occupied Lithuania. She even worked three jobs at one point to support us. She taught me in early childhood to be an independent woman and never rely on a man.

My early twenties were highly influenced by my early childhood. We did not have much financially. I watched my alcoholic father abuse my mother physically then finally witnessed their divorce. I then watched my hard-working mother struggle to support two children on her own. Despite the tough childhood, I always knew that I was loved unconditionally by my parents and my family. As an early teenager, I was already growing up to be a very independent woman. I wanted to live on my own, as soon as possible, and needed to build a life without my parents' financial support, but in the early 2000s, my choices in Lithuanian were limited.

When I was only twenty years old, I left Lithuania for London, England in order, to seek better economic opportunities for myself. I had no friends and no English language skills, which limited the jobs I could get in London. Yet in only a few years I managed to excel and get to a manager's position in a boutique restaurant in the financial district of Cheapside. I was making decent money while my Lithuanian husband at the time was getting into alcoholism and was super jealous of my career and the ease in which I was assimilating into English society. Our marriage was going south and one day I had to fend for myself in a locked bathroom while my husband was beating me. I attempted to climb out of the window, which unfortunately made things physically worse for me.

Several hours after this incident, I told myself that no man, for any reason, will raise a hand against me ever again! Although I witnessed my mom take repeated beatings from my dad, I was not her, and I was committed this was it! I left my husband and found myself homeless, crashing on my friends' couches for a while until I found my own place. My strong belief in myself and self-respect drove me to succeed, and I committed to never falling weak and going back to him, regardless of how often he chased me to get me back. On a funny note, he got me 100 gorgeous red long stem roses as an apology and asked to get back together. The roses did not change my mind about leaving him. When I told him that, he clipped each rose off his stem with the scissors as a sign of grief.

I was stronger mentally than ever before, knowing there is no price for freedom.

Fast forward 15 years and I was living in Seattle, Washington. I was coming out of another failed marriage. I had graduated from the University of Washington with a degree in International Studies and was now working at an amazing software company offering solutions to the logistics industry. I felt blessed with more life learning experiences that made me appreciate the good and the bad, because all of it created me – an independent woman, who loves what she does and finally living life on my own terms. I felt free and the last thing I wanted was another relationship or marriage.

Until I met the love of my life – Tarl Yarber. We both are stubborn, independent people who like our freedom. At first, we put each other through six harsh months of games. We both acted as if we did not want to be in a relationship, yet we could not be away from each other for more than a day or two at the most. In the end, we let down our guards, and fell deeply in love.

Soon we were two fiercely independent people, happily married, respecting each other's independent personalities and different career paths. I was happy working in the software business and Tarl was just as content with his successful real estate investment business flipping single-family residential homes. Originally, I did not want anything to do with real estate, however, after witnessing the freedom Tarl had to travel and attend real estate conferences nationwide, I changed my mind. Long hours were keeping me away from Tarl and prohibiting me from traveling with him. The catalyst that sealed my desire to transition to real estate was when we kept some of our flips as rentals. While working at my job, I managed the rentals. At that moment I realized what real estate could offer to our family; more time together, and the freedom to do what we wanted to do, when we wanted to do it. To get there, we would need to build more passive cash flow by adding more single-family rentals to our portfolio.

At the end of 2017, I was at a crossroads: do I join Tarl in real estate, or do I continue working in the software business I loved, which provided me my lifelong goal of financial independence. I struggled with this decision, as due to my past, I did not want to rely on him. Ultimately, I wanted to know my lane in his real estate business before I would make the transition.

Before understanding my position in Tarl's company, we allocated a weekend to map out our ideal life. Then we looked at what businesses (and revenue streams) would fit that lifestyle. That weekend forever changed our lives and our thinking.

Today, we are no longer consumed, like most societies, who fit their personal lives around the time left over from working; we fit work around our personal lives. To do this, we simply first made the decision we were not happy spending so little time with each other, and then second, made a plan that supported us in solving that problem.

To think it took only two days of planning to achieve the life of our dreams in less than 6 months!! The vehicle that made this all possible was real estate. We have heard it said countless times, but now we were living it!

Today, I serve as the property manager for our rental portfolio. I also assist our real estate events' business too. To build my knowledge base about property management, I listened to podcasts, read articles, attended local meetups and met with other landlords. In the first year, we acquired twelve single-family home rentals with close to zero money down.

Our real estate business can operate from afar through just our cell phones. In both 2018 and 2019, we spent 229 days traveling together! This is not by accident; this is exactly what we planned that one weekend in 2017.

Besides traveling, serving our community, friends and helping those in need are also a big part of our lives. We realize these goals through our events' business. Our local meet-up "Fixated On Real Estate," in WA, approximately 150 people each month. These monthly events provide investors the ability to network, educate and empower each other. We are planning to expand our meetups to other states. Besides our meet-up, we host the largest annual conference on the west coast called "PNW Big Badass Real Estate Wealth Expo." This is a multi-day event that brings in 1000+ attendees, with over 40+ speakers and over 50+ vendors.

They say be careful what you wish for, it might come true...and in our case it did. After extensively traveling for a few years, we learned that we are longing to be home. We have shifted our focus to grow our real estate business and our events' business, start a family and get a puppy. To date, the past few years of spending more time together were the most fulfilling years of our lives. We may have made less money during that time, than when we were both working full-time, but we were rich in life.

Grace Yarber

Grace Yarber believes that anything is possible in life if one puts all his/her efforts into it. Born in Lithuania to loving parents during the Soviet Occupation, adversity and scarce times taught her to have extreme gratitude for the simple things in life. She came to the United States in 2005 to build her own American Dream, which included freedom of choice, equality and prosperity. Grace began her career in the food and beverage industry, and after getting her education in the United States, she transitioned to software sales for the logistics industry. Now she uses those same skills to help manage and run a very successful single-family real estate portfolio and events business in the Seattle-area alongside her loving husband, Tarl.

Ultimate happiness was created in 2017, when Grace and her husband mapped out the lifestyle of their dreams and fitted their business around that lifestyle. In 2018 and 2019, she was able to travel 229 days with her husband, all while running their business remotely. Grace enjoys hiking, snowboarding, reading, gardening, paddle boarding, salsa dancing, tennis, playing with her dog Duke and is also scared of bugs. Grace is passionate about helping others overcome their fears and limiting beliefs. Excited about life, she wishes nothing more than to share that excitement with others and leave a positive impact on the people around her she cares most about.

Wasting Youth on Real Estate
by Brittany Arnason

Wealth is a tool that gives you choices–but does not
compensate for a life fully lived.
-Oprah Winfrey

According to GEM statistics, more than 41% of people aged 25-34, who consider becoming entrepreneurs are held back due to the fear of failure. With only 18% of entrepreneurs finding success, regardless of age, fear of failure is a warranted emotion. Despite all of this, there are some huge advantages to following your passion and starting a business at a young age. Before I dive into them, let me start by telling you my story.

Jumping into real estate full time at only 24 years old, I had a million questions. I kept thinking of what the worst-case scenario would be. What if I totally screw up? My answer: I would just get another job or go back to school. Not a big deal, I knew I could handle it, but for some reason that question kept resurfacing. As I continued to push through my self-doubt, I would remind myself that trying this path I felt passionate about was much better than working any job for where I felt no purpose.

Lemons to Lemonade

I never went to university. Not attending university created a limited belief I was not smart enough. When I stand next to my peers, I always wonder, by not attending university, am I at a deficit? It only takes me a second to realize the answer. *I am the youngest person in the room because I did not go to university.* The advantage I have is that I never had looming student loan debt governing the investment decisions I could make. Instead, I worked extremely hard, always with multiple jobs and used my money to invest.

Today I am known for doing EVERYTHING in my investing business. The term *Do it yourself*, or DIY, is often used to describe this. This is another example of how I was able to turn a negative into a positive. All renovations boil down to two components: time and money. Unless you have a huge margin, one of those components is always sacrificed for the other. In my situation, I sacrificed time to do my projects cheaper, because frankly, I did not have the funds, nor did the project allow for it. This forced me to learn everything from scratch. While taking this approach held me back at first, today it has propelled my success to a level I could not imagine. And, to be honest, I absolutely love doing it!

Getting Started

When I was six years old, I was at a restaurant for a Christmas party, and I, along with everyone else there, got food poisoning from undercooked food. Little did I know that this single event set the stage for my investing career. The restaurant ended up compensating everyone for this terrible situation, I received $15,000. Fast forward 12 years later, I was 18 years old and bought my first rental property for $25,000. Could you say I was out of my comfort zone, yes...I was terrified.

Comfort Zone

A lot of my life has occurred outside of my comfort zone. It is not always a fun place to be. Typically, I have had moments of regret and question if I should give up or back out. I ultimately stuck it out, and EVERY single time I am so happy I did. Some of these situations include buying my first few properties, renovating properties alone, traveling the world solo by backpacking in countries where I didn't speak the language, shark cage diving, bungee jumping, skydiving (if you are comfortable doing these things, are you even human?), speaking in front of investors at conferences and speaking on podcasts. ALL these things terrified me, and a lot of it still does. I have spent countless nights crying on the floor stressed out because I have no idea what I am doing, feeling stupid and scared. However, ALL of this, once conquered, makes me so incredibly proud and happy.

Ask and You Shall Receive

A lot of these opportunities have come from asking for them, putting myself out there and working hard for exactly what I wanted. My motto in life is "if you don't ask, you don't receive." Simply asking for something has provided a lot of opportunities and has really surprised me in some cases. I am relentless for getting or doing something I want. If I get ignored or rejected when I first ask, guess what, I keep trying.

One example of this is when I bought my fourth property. The bank would not give me a loan because of the size of the town and the low price of the property ($40,000). I then asked everyone I could think of, mortgage brokers, banks, etc. until I found a banker who said, "I cannot give you a mortgage, but I can give you a line of credit for $50,000." Secretly excited, I said, "Well, that is good, but I think I will need a bit more because I am doing renovations and you never know what could come up." He said, "Ok, I understand. How about $75,000?"

CHA-CHING! This single line of credit has allowed me to do so much in real estate...much more than just purchase and renovate my fourth property. I have used it to purchase properties, fix them up, and once refinanced through my partner, repeat over and over again!

Just think, if I was not pushed to that uncomfortable point (not having financing from my typical source), coupled with my relentless tenacity to keep asking for something I want, I most likely would not even be here writing this chapter.

Do It Yourself

One reason I love being a DIY real estate investor. By literally doing all aspects you learn quickly what you do and do not love to do. Knowing both is very important. Specifically, I discovered property management, bookkeeping and working through the details are not for me. However, I find great joy in big picture thinking, deal hunting, renovation work design and networking.

One of the things I love the most is DIY renovations. I enjoy this because it 1) saves money, 2) gives you time to learn by listening to books and podcasts 3) you are less likely to get taken advantage of because it gives you an understanding of the process. Like anything, there are disadvantages too. Some examples are 1) difficulty in scaling the business, 2) the time it takes to learn a new skill and 3) the overall investment in the tools needed to complete the job. If you enjoy doing DIY projects, remember you do not have to do an entire house DIY. Instead, start with a few small projects and see how you do and feel; you may surprise yourself.

Put Yourself Out There

A major contributing factor in my success thus far has been creating an online presence through social media, specifically my Instagram page @InvestorGirlBritt. I share everything I am going through as a young investor, the good, the bad and the ugly. I do my best to share my daily life, lessons learned and hard times. I love to help other people through my videos, whether that's inspiring them to get their hands dirty through renovations or investing in real estate in general.

Three factors contributing to my drive to post online were; the freedom to travel, some of my high school friends were doing this and making money online (the initial reason I started my online presence), to prove myself to everyone who doubted me and to create credibility for myself as a real estate investor. All these reasons kept me consistent in growing my personal brand and have directly contributed to where I am today.

Finding Purpose and Direction

I always thought real estate would be a vehicle to take me from my passion to financial freedom. During my journey, there were opinions and distractions making me question if I could only find success by fitting into the preconceived notion of a real estate investor. Fortunately, I found a love and joy in working the day-to-day operations I did not expect. It is when I harnessed my creative self, seeing my ideas come to life through my renovation work, I found my success. I learned it does not always have to be how much money you make, or how many doors you have, set your goals, make smart investment decisions and stay true to yourself. If you follow these principles, wealth will follow.

Y.O.Y.O. You're Only Young Once

George Bernard Shaw is famously quoted as saying, "Youth is wasted on the young." That may be true for a lot of people, but I am doing the opposite; I am maximizing it. As a young entrepreneur there are a lot of advantages. While there is an inevitable fear of failure, mistakes come quicker and allow you the opportunity to learn faster. You also have more time to find purpose and direction. When you are young, it is easier to live extremely cheap (like how I do living in my converted school bus or work van). Another advantage is not having high overhead, like a house, kids and debt.

Like everything, there are some disadvantages too. As a young entrepreneur, your access to capital and networks is limited. To combat the capital issue start working another job and create your business on the side. Then share your story through social media, and you will build your own network, solving the second problem that comes along with youth. This is exactly what I did, and surprisingly the money and opportunities followed.

My advice to you is to get started as soon as possible. No one will ever be able to give you all the answers and you probably will never feel ready, you just must give it a shot. I promise you it will be hard; I know this firsthand as I have wanted to give up many times. Most investors do give up and I DO NOT WANT YOU TO BE THAT PERSON.

Build a network of people that not only provides knowledge, but also supports you when you face adversity. I am very fortunate to have a supportive family and group of friends. My support network gets me through some pretty bad situations. Despite whatever I have gone through, or will go through, there is someone dealing with an even worse situation. Ultimately your mindset determines whether a situation can be overcome. People of all ages can determine their mindset; just like real estate, your age is not a limitation.

Brittany Arnason

Brittany, also known as Investor Girl Britt, grew up in a beautiful mountain town of Canmore, Alberta, always taking advantage of outdoor activities such as hiking and snowboarding. After high school, she spent a few years backpacking solo around the world, her passion for being a nomad and not wanting to be tied down propelled her into real estate as she was not interested in the 9-5 lifestyle. She bought her first house at 18 years old and jumped into real estate investing full-time at 24. Her focus is long-term buy and hold rental properties, and her portfolio consists of single families, duplexes, apartments and (most recently) self-storage facilities. Her creativity and passion shine through by designing and doing the renovation work on her properties, she is not afraid to tackle any project from demo to the finishing stage. Sharing this process online, she helps inspire others to find what they love and do the same. By putting herself out there, it has given her a platform to speak on stages across North America, TV Shows, Magazines, podcasts and YouTube videos. Real estate investing has given her freedom, flexibility and she is so grateful to be on this path she loves and gets to teach others how to do the same. You can follow Brittany on Instagram @InvestorGirlBritt.

Reinventing Yourself
by Patricia L. Red Hawk, MD

Sometimes change comes at you, like a broadside accident...
-Joni Mitchell

Sometimes failure sends you indirectly toward success. In my case, despite making it as far as graduating medical school and grinding through countless hours of studying, I had failed my medical boards' exam. Again.

I did eventually pass, earning my MD, but this constant struggle made me wonder if it was all worth it. Where did being a doctor, who carved her way into that noble profession, and then made her way out, lead me? How did I even get from there to here? Writing this chapter has allowed me to revisit my crazy, challenging and circuitous route to financial freedom. I will show you how I survived a crushing career blow, reinvented myself, found true love and ultimately chose new pathways forward—still landing on my feet. Most importantly, I hope to show you exactly how it can be done...how you can take my lessons learned and apply them to your own life.

It can be said of real estate investors that we are all self-taught. We have extensive libraries of dog-eared books, numerous podcast favorites we listen to weekly and website forums in which we faithfully participate. While it is true, we are all self-taught, but none of us are self-*made*. And, that point is even more salient when you are a woman.

Every successful woman real estate investor I know has asked for help, and, most importantly given it. It is a uniquely curious and giving community, this one of females helping females. I have been fortunate to have successful mentors climb the ladder with one hand while reaching the other back to take mine.

Now allow me to reach back for yours.

Nobody Starts off Right

I grew up in the San Francisco Bay area during the '70s, at the "headwaters" of Silicon Valley. In many respects, I was in the right place at the right time, but it certainly didn't feel like that growing up (does it ever for anyone)? I am an only child and grew up with a single mom (although dad was somewhat in the picture, he lived for most of my childhood in Canada).

My dad was a classic salesman with tons of bonhomie and grandiose ideas masquerading as an ambition but could never actually execute any of his plans. At some point in his adult career, my dad pivoted from salesman to a real estate broker. He managed to white-knuckle his way through two California market downturns and finally decided he had had enough. He finished his career as a civil servant, working as a master appraiser for the Sonoma County Assessor's Office.

In retrospect, I see that my father possessed tremendous social IQ but was stunted emotionally. Dad was a bully and a misogynist, too. He had problematic relationships with every meaningful female in his life, including me. When I came out of the closet at age nineteen, my dad took me for a drive through the Sierra Nevada foothills. During that long and painful ride, he told me I was sick, broken and insisted something was wrong with me. I do not know why I did not believe him, why I did not internalize his judgments—in fact, I remember thinking, "this is total bullshit."

Through the years, my dad would manufacture some pretense to be angry with me and we would carry on being estranged for a period. This went on intermittently for many years, never gaining resolution. Dad could not accept having a lesbian for a daughter, despite my many other accomplishments. He died alone in 2014, during one of these estrangements.

My mom bootstrapped her way out of a post-Depression-era poverty by attending a two-year nursing program and worked as a registered nurse for the rest of her life. She was a steady worker: dependable, conscientious, and committed, but not ambitious.

I am an adult child of an alcoholic parent. My mom started to abuse alcohol when I was about nine years old and was a full-blown drunk by the time I was twelve. As her nightly drinking episodes became more abusive, her daytime memory loss and attempts at gaslighting became more fervent. It was just the two of us in my house growing up, making me the only witness to my own abuse. She remained a drunk for the rest of her life, ironically washing down her life-saving medicines with vodka while in hospice care during the months before she died in 2016.

Tragic struggles aside, my parents both loved me and contributed to my life in many important ways. From my mother, I learned the value of security, of a steady paycheck and a "good job with benefits." Mom learned those Depression-era lessons well and ingrained them into me. From my father, I learned the power of humor and of social interactions, and of how to harness "the gift of gab." However, neither of my parents were able to recognize or elevate most of my unique, innate gifts. I am not sure if they even saw them in themselves. I think we were better off than many, but behind the scenes, we struggled.

Many families endure challenges—alcoholism, financial issues, job changes, relocation, divorce—but growing up with parents who taught you about building wealth is not required for you to build wealth. So, do not use this as an excuse to not get your ass off the couch!

Lessons Learned - Childhood

- Know your own truth
- Find your center, stay true to it
- Feel the fear, do it anyway

I am grateful for my intellect. It has served me well and brought me far. It has helped me tackle new subjects, learn new skills and embrace new ideas. But if we are completely honest here, attaining real wealth and financial freedom does not actually require great intelligence. It requires action.

Anyone can attain what I and the other authors have: the financial freedom to do what we want, when we want, where we want and with whomever we want. The difference between those who embrace the lessons offered in this book and do something and those who do not is simple; they do something.

What the Hell Are You Waiting For??

Many years ago, now, I was working with a therapist to help get out from underneath the psychological damage associated with my alcoholic mother. My counselor suggested that I seek to increase my self-confidence, but how? I had no real idea how anyone did this, "take risks" she said. And she was right.

Of course, now, with the benefit of decades of life experience and plenty of risk-taking along the way, I understand exactly what she meant. Today, many people ask me to coach or mentor them. Since I love to teach, this is a fun opportunity for me to share my experience, knowledge, wisdom and insights with other smart, ambitious, opportunity-seeking people. But the truth is this—*most people never take action.* The first thing I do when someone expresses interest in working with me is to assign them homework. The homework is not complicated or time-consuming. Every successful investor I know has already done it. Yet I can count on one hand the number of "newbies" who have completed the assignment.

Not everyone who asks me for coaching is necessarily a good fit. I want my students to acquire new knowledge, understand how to apply it, and execute their own plan and finally, be held accountable for their progress. It can be a deeply rewarding experience, but only if they are willing to act.

So, here's the real deal, it's not enough to *want it*—you must *go after it.* Acting will stop whatever emotional or mental pain is associated with remaining in your current state. You can only obtain results when you act—which differs from being in motion. Even now, I think I'm being productive when I'm just busy, not the same thing. How do you know the difference? Acting yields results and merely being in motion does not.

As soon as I started to act and really push myself, I discovered a whole treasure of personal insights, talents and gifts I possess. I promise, if you act in your own life, you will too. Along the way, you will also stop complaining, blaming others, overcome fear, develop new skills, boost your personal satisfaction in life, gain the respect of others, minimize regrets in life and oh yeah, build real wealth. *Real wealth.*

Wherever You Are Now, Get Started

I had the usual collection of ridiculous jobs as a young adult: restaurant worker, snack bar attendant, telemarketer, pool cleaner—even a stint as a tour boat guide at Marine World/Africa USA! (For those of you who know where the Oracle corporate HQ is in California, it sits atop that former jungle animal/water ski show park.)

After surviving a head-on collision in my 20's, I endured a long rehab period wherein I had plenty of time to consider what could happen next in my life. It makes me laugh now to consider my thought process then: "Men earn a lot more money...what do men do for jobs?"

I considered a few options. Since I learned some basic construction drawing/drafting skills in high school, I hustled my way into a job working for a general contractor (GC). There were three female GCs in the Women's Business Yellow Pages. I called all three, but only one picked up the phone. From them, I landed drafting and labor jobs. Ultimately, I learned carpentry and residential remodeling. From this job, I met a group of male thirty-somethings who were flipping houses in San Jose's Almaden Valley. These guys were doing this before it was even called "flipping." My first taste of real estate investing were these small-house, simple flip projects. (More on that later.)

The public school system in California was robust in the '70s. At one point there were more community colleges in California than in all forty-nine other states combined. If you wanted a college education in this place at this time, by George, you could get one, and I did.

My public high school was better than average. Even though my own family was not middle-class, the surrounding area was. Fortunately, I benefited from the classic middle-class expectations about going to college and having a career. What emerged as the real challenge though, was how to pay for it. Even though both my parents vaguely supported the idea of me attending college, neither of them offered to pay for it. Not a single dime. So, I bootstrapped my way through college and paid for it myself. Well, me and Uncle Sam. Given the cost of college with no family financial support, I enlisted in the California Army National Guard. The GI Bill provided just the money I needed, and I remain grateful to this day it was available. While it did not cover the entire cost, it covered enough I could work full-time to support myself and make ends meet.

My major area of study at San Jose State University was Industrial Design aka Product Design. I loved it but found the environment to be so overwhelmingly male that it never seemed like there was room for me as a woman. I do not even remember there being any other women in the Industrial Design Program.

Lessons Learned

- Grow your self-confidence by taking risks
- Be open to new things—opportunities, adventures, skills, people
- Course-correct if needed
- Don't be swayed by others' opinions of your new ideas/directions (it reflects them and their world, not you and yours)
- Never take a job for the paycheck; intentionally choose a job because you want to learn new skills, have new experiences, work with certain people, enjoy growth opportunities (e.g., US Army for the GI bill)

Off to War

In August of 1990, Saddam Hussein of Iraq invaded neighboring Kuwait. My girlfriend at the time and I remarked on it as we made coffee and listened to NPR. As the situation continued to develop over the following weeks, the possibility of my Army National Guard unit being mobilized to active duty became increasingly real until it happened. I received orders to active duty to support Operation Desert Storm. It all happened in a whirlwind—my girlfriend took my dog, I moved out of my house, withdrew from my university, stepped away from my construction job, and put my life on hold—hoping I'd come back to it all.

There were many things I remember clearly about the time I served in the Middle East. My battalion provided Military Police to an Enemy Prisoner of War camp, deep in the desert. Since I worked the night shift, I spent many hours looking up at that inky black sky punctuated with stars brighter than I had ever seen. It was a time of deep contemplation for me. I asked myself, "If I die here, what would I regret?" I would regret I never embraced my long-held desire to be a doctor. I had wanted to be a physician for many years, but that was for rich kids—kids whose parents went to college and knew how to guide them, not for kids like me. It was a subtle shift over months, but one night, while lying on my back on top of the gravity-fed water tower that provided our showers, I first said out loud, "I'm going to be a doctor." When I returned home and told friends and family, I got...*CRICKETS*.

There were only a few people who believed in me, but that was fine. I had hustle and I had grit. I got my ass off the couch.

Lessons Learned

- Determine the cost of attaining your dream before committing. When you commit, resolve to pay the price without wavering
- Be relentless
- There is always someone smarter/better than you—just make sure nobody can "out-hustle" you. Grind more than others! The "scorched earth" approach

Paging Dr. Red Hawk

I worked exceptionally hard to get through my undergraduate degree —both the scientific material as well as the logistics of doing so while working full-time. I thought that attending school during the weekdays and working the second shift until 12:30 AM all week long was hard enough.... (med school: "Here: hold my beer!").

Becoming a physician is an amazing, humbling, arduous and excruciating process. Whatever you understand about yourself prior to med school will be challenged. Whatever equilibrium you possess will be rocked.

And not for nothing. Making a doctor is part education, part alchemy. The magic that happens between doctor and patient is sacred. I enjoyed caring for patients and their families; it was deeply gratifying work. However, I found the business of medicine to be burdensome because the American healthcare system is broken. The ultimate understatement.

My academic successes in medical school were sporadic, but an interesting pattern emerged. When I was graded on clinical work—which included relational and social components, plus the ability to "workshop" (problem-solve in real-time with colleagues) the medical information—I performed exceptionally well. I earned Honors in virtually all my clinical rotation assessments. However, my scores on national standardized exams were consistently abysmal. I struggled to pass my USMLE medical board exams, repeating them multiple times until I squeaked out a passing grade.

Lessons Learned - Temple University School of Medicine

- Stay humble
- Take a team approach whenever you can (All of You are always better than Just You)
- Embrace the details—the How of something, the Why of something and how you can affect it (what levers to pull/push). Know all the "knowable" information—then ask yourself, "Does this change my direction or path?"
- Know your weaknesses well; your strengths will take care of themselves

Complications and Resolutions

Many years later, my wife (a preschool teacher) suggested I be tested. She insisted, "You are brilliant, but something is not working right for you." Sure enough, after a long day in Manhattan and many hours of testing, the physician explained my learning disability. Everything clicked and so many of my past academic challenges were explained.

Today, I employ a whole arsenal of processing tools to help me maximize my thinking and productivity. I am grateful my wife pushed me to get tested, but also sad when I consider what could have been had someone in medical school suggested testing me.

In 2010, I had failed Step 3 of my USMLE boards and I stepped away from clinical medicine altogether. It was heartbreaking. Becoming a physician had been my sole goal, spanning twenty years of hopes and dreams. It cost me a tremendous amount of money, time, sweat, blood and more than a few tears.

But I was done.

Lessons Learned

- It became obvious that a disability was blocking progress in my career (and would always be a struggle for me) because I consistently struggled to pass national exams
- My med school grades illustrated to me that my operational strengths are relational and social, and that I do best by "workshopping" information
- Learn where you need support and get it early

Now What?

I had been laser-focused on medicine for so long, I was not sure what else I wanted to do or could do. I was forty-seven, divorced, with shared custody of my young son. It seemed a ridiculous idea to go back to school for some other career. I needed a new direction and one that would not cost me more money or time. I needed to both reinvent myself and retool simultaneously, and I needed to do it right now.

I took a few years to consider my options. And while I did some special project work and consulting to make ends meet, I had the time to consider what I enjoyed doing and what previous work I liked in the past. Ultimately, it was my medical practice that informed my new direction. When my patients lived in low-quality or transient housing, the quality of their entire life suffered. Their relationships, occupations, finances—everything was compromised when their housing was inadequate or poor.

As I considered this idea and what my new role in the community could look like, I remembered the fun I had designing remodeling projects and working with the "flipping guys" in San Jose. Once the idea took hold, it was easy to connect the dots for me.

At heart, I am an entrepreneur. I see opportunity everywhere and relish the "what if" process of development. Over the years, I had accumulated dozens of books on real estate investing. I dug them out again to consume and study the vocabulary, tactics and strategies. The extreme volume of material and pace of medical school is often described as trying to "drink from a firehose"—but it was a skill set I had mastered; I knew how to learn!

Lessons Learned - Pivot or Persevere

- Re: Clinical Medicine, "Why am I working so hard for a career I no longer am committed to pursuing?"

- What work did I previously enjoy?
- Design, construction, marketing, small business, entrepreneurship - what about these resonated for me?
- Can I engage in these topics now?

Get Your Ass off the Couch

Today when I speak about my real estate investing career, I emphasize the need for constant and ongoing learning. My typical week includes 15-20 hours of podcasts that I listen to while I drive around in my truck. There is also a stack of relevant books on my nightstand. To be a successful investor you absolutely must become a lifelong learner. Markets cycle up and down, vary by locale, and all against the backdrop of larger market forces. You must be prepared with both a broad and deep fund of knowledge to chart a path of success.

As I write this chapter, our country is gripped by the developing COVID-19 pandemic—a true economic "black swan" if ever there was one. My constant studying and research led me to make significant structural changes in my company and in my portfolio, beginning in the fall of 2019. It is not that I saw this specific pandemic coming, but rather I came to believe that the global credit market and our country's own economic markets and monetary policy are riddled with a financial cancer that is terminal. We are experiencing an enormous economic shift and I intend to mitigate risks while optimizing profits and researching new opportunities.

Lessons Learned

- Learn to reverse engineer what you want in life and choose your own adventure

- Ask yourself: What does my perfect day look like at work? With my family? What do I want to accomplish/experience in my life? What do I need to make these things happen (most likely time and/or money)? In my case, I wanted the freedom to pursue fun and meaningful activities, money to support myself and my endeavors, control over my income streams and more security than the stock market
- Ask yourself: What steps are needed to get to my goal?
- Take inventory: What are my current resources (financial, relational, time)? Supplement with what you are lacking (knowledge, money, time, skills, people, systems and processes)
- Show your work! Can someone review your plan? Ask for help from someone already doing what you want to do—DO NOT ask advice from anyone NOT doing it

Hustle and Grit, Both Are Required

Do you remember at the beginning of this chapter when I said, "We are all self-taught but none of us is self-made?" It's true. The freedom, success, security and wealth obtained by investing in real estate is incredible. Investing in real estate is simple. (Trust me, it's not nearly as hard as being a medical doctor!)

Yes, I said real estate investing is *simple* and it is, but that doesn't mean it's easy. Real estate investing is hard as hell, and at times you will need every ounce of strength you have to persevere.

Hustle will get you to the table, but grit allows you to keep it.

If you reflect on your own life and find times when you had to work hard and relentlessly focus on a goal, despite some discomfort--you've got hustle. If you know how to work with a sense of urgency and purpose, you've got hustle. And hustle will get you a very long way, but it cannot keep you there--only grit can do that.

When you are the only woman in the room, or only queer person, or the only person of color--you will need grit too. Displaying grit will look like courage, dependability, confidence, creativity, optimism and most importantly, resilience. Grit is the drive to persevere and achieve. The more you display it, the more you will have.

"Well Ya' See Timmy..."

Most of you are not old enough to remember the old Lassie movies or TV shows, I barely do. Like so many American shows, they were heavy-handed and formulaic with whatever "moral of the story" was being conveyed. In the final scene, some characters would always drive the point home with a "well ya' see Timmy, it's like this..." episode-ending dialogue.

I wrote my chapter to include many of the challenges and obstacles I encountered along the way because I wanted you to see my pivot points. There are times in my life where I have reinvented myself to adapt, adjust and overcome obstacles. It's easy to talk yourself out of doing the hard work, the homework. But if you have hustle and grit, if you will be relentless about educating yourself and persevering regardless of circumstances, you will achieve a destiny that few ever do.

Dr. Patricia Red Hawk

Dr. Red Hawk is an award-winning residential remodeler and experienced real estate investor with dozens of projects completed. She is a true "utility player" with a broad skill set in the investment space utilizing multiple strategies including BRRRR, Fix-and-Flip, Value Add/Forced Appreciation and Wholesaling to great success.

Born and raised in the San Francisco Bay Area, she put herself through college while also serving in the California Army National Guard. After a tour of duty in the Middle East, she moved to Philadelphia to attend Temple University School of Medicine, training in Family Medicine.

Today Dr. Red Hawk is a full-time real estate investor and business owner, living with her wife and kids in the Pacific Northwest. She swims a mile a day, enjoys riding motorcycles, painting, sailing, teaching investing/wealth building and great BBQ. Every February she is heard to say, "…maybe this is the year I buy a sailboat…".

For more information-
www.PatriciaRedHawkMD.com
www.linkedin.com/in/patriciaredhawk
Instagram: @RedHawkMD

Getting Started
by Deborah Nye

The best way to predict the future is to create it.
—Abraham Lincoln

"YOU ARE NUTS!" If someone had told me ten years ago that today I would have a multi-million-dollar real estate portfolio, be teaching about real estate investing, be part of a book, and writing my own, that is what I would have said. Absolutely, totally, nuts.

Here I am, over ten years later and I can honestly say all of that came to be true. If I can do it, so can you! Sure, lots of people say that. Here's where I differ-I'll SHOW you how! Read on.

The amazing thing about Real Estate is your background does not matter. Your education does not matter. Your age does not matter. Your financial situation does not matter. Your current circumstances do not matter. What matters is your ability to ***build a team, educate yourself, have a goal, and act.*** The specifics of any new endeavor can feel overwhelming, but if you focus on these four things, you can, rather, you **will** succeed.

My Beginning

Looking back, it isn't surprising that I got into real estate given the impression my father made on me. My dad was always renovating our houses while we lived in them. I watched how he would install tile (wet bed!) without spacers and his grout lines would be perfectly even. We were the only family that owned a multi-unit apartment building and had tenants. My dad and I would chat with his tenants and I would keep my dad company while he did repairs. My education in tenants and toilets had begun.

After graduating from RISD (Rhode Island School of Design), I found myself always improving the places where I lived. For example, I would install a new tile floor in the bathroom, new cabinets in the kitchen, maybe paint interesting colors. However, it wasn't until 2008 when I could renovate a whole house I wasn't living in. Before the financial crash my husband had a friend, who was about to lose his property to foreclosure. The property was a small two-bedroom row house that needed significant renovation. I went on Angie's list, found a plumber (who had a helper) and we completed that little house in about six weeks with virtually no problems. How can you not be hooked after an experience like that!? I acted and was on my way to building a team.

Build a Team

For your first step toward building a team, give a thought to who you use for repairs around your own house. Talk to these service people. Talk to your electrician. Talk to your plumber. Ask if they do whole house renovations and would be interested in helping you with your next renovation project. Ask them about prices. Ask them for recommendations for other tradespeople; for example, painters and landscapers. While going about your day, pay attention to the service vans of tradespeople you see, jot down numbers or take a picture of the vans with the company names. Join the Nextdoor app. Go to www.nextdoor.com where you will find your neighborhood group that helps build your community and is great for referrals.

Educate Yourself

I wanted to keep renovating properties, but I knew little about the business, especially since the first one fell into my lap. I joined a local real estate investment group. I networked; I took classes. I got so bogged down with various acquisition techniques I didn't buy another property for three years. However, I became a real estate agent. I reasoned that becoming an agent and having MLS (multiple listing service) access would increase my chances of finding properties. Guess what? It worked. The next few properties I bought were straight from the MLS. Being a Realtor has not only given me access to information, but also has given me additional income.

Go to www.nationalreia.org (National Real Estate Investment Association, NREIA). Find a group near you. Go to a meeting. Start to network. Take classes. Don't have time? Go to the group's website and watch webinars. Groups across the country offer webinars that you can access just for being a National REIA member. You will also find other networking groups specific to real estate only in your area. Don't forget to enlist realtors to help educate you and help you find properties. They are a valuable part of any team. If you are looking in more than one area, do not hesitate to find more than one realtor, each realtor will know each specific area and help you learn it too.

Have a Goal

I did not have any property acquisition goals, nor any financial ones. I was just seeing where this property stuff would go. My strategy was to buy, renovate, rent, refinance and repeat. Today this method is famously known as "BRRRR."

Although I was very comfortable with my strategy, after all, it was working, I had an aha moment when I attended an REIA meeting where the topic was *having a goal*. (Thank you, Marc Halpern,) Marc posed a simple question to the audience, "Do you need money now? Do you need money in 5 years? Or do you need money for retirement?" He discussed how different strategies can meet each goal. For example, money for retirement can be achieved by the cash flow from rentals. If you need money sooner, flipping or wholesaling could provide quick cash.

After that meeting, I realized my goal: *Creating enough money for retirement*. Although I had positive cash flow from my properties, when I considered my age and the rate at which I was acquiring properties, I realized I needed a much quicker way to increase the income. So, I pivoted. Specifically, I sought *higher-yielding* cash flowing properties. I bought a couple of student rentals, a "rent by the room" property, a medical office building and an apartment building in another state. With each purchase, I upped my game using the techniques I had learned from all those classes. The result? Once I focused on my goal, I didn't need *as many* properties!

What Is *Your* Goal?

So, ask yourself, what do you really need? You may already be set with retirement funds. Maybe your full-time job earns you a nice living. Do you *need* to have $100M in property in ten years? If so, great, go for it! Is it a personal game to see what you can achieve? That's fine too. Maybe you just want some extra income, or to establish an inheritance for your children. Set realistic goals and don't feel demoralized if you aren't $100M ambitious. Whatever the goal, there is a way through real estate to achieve that goal.

Take Action!

Go find a property. Still have no idea how to do that? Do you have a cell phone or a computer? Call or email every contact you have and tell them you are looking for an investment property. Ask them who they know that could help. Then follow-up with them monthly. Want more ways? Buy a list, do direct mail, put up bandit signs, go to Meet-Ups, network, and don't forget realtors. Get out there and knock on some doors! Introduce yourself, give the homeowner a takeaway with what you are about and your contact information.

You do not need to be too specific with a certain technique (for example: buying only foreclosures, or only doing lease-options). When there is so little inventory, we can't be so specific with buying criteria. Instead *focus on the property*. Initially, I had no plan for how I bought or when, I just looked for ways to make that specific property work for making a good return. My first property was on its way to foreclosure, but I didn't exclude other types of property.

Now FIND THE MONEY to purchase it. There are only TWO ways to finance the purchase of a property, YOUR MONEY or OTHER PEOPLE'S MONEY. That is it. I have used my money. I have used other people's money, including; bank money, construction loans, private money, self-directed IRA money. I would even use "hard" money if I needed it. My first property was bought by a conventional mortgage. I put 20% down and financed the rest. I used my own cash to renovate it. Eventually, I refinanced it and got my cashback.

While working on financing, determining the "exit strategy" for the property will help tremendously. Will it be a rental, or will you fix and sell it? Either way, I suggest enlisting a realtor to help. In finding a tenant, a realtor offers expertise and will cut down your learning curve. You will get a better qualified and screened tenant. Using an agent to sell the property will yield you a bucket load more than doing it yourself, up to 23% more, according to the National Association of Realtors.

Do you *need* to fix up the property? View other properties in your market. Work the numbers and find the best option. Finding contractors isn't that difficult. Keeping good contractors is the hard part. Paint stores, plumbing supply stores and electrical supply stores have community boards where tradespeople post their business cards. You can even ask the store employees for their recommendations. Try Angie's list. That's how I got started. That and my REIA.

One Last Tip

As a woman in this business, we are often overlooked. Once, I had a contractor ask to speak with my husband, or my project manager, when I asked him for a quote. Although it can be challenging at times, let none of this type of interaction derail you. I did not let it derail me, no successful woman will. Lots of components will help you succeed;

including the support of your significant other, friends and family, the ability to seek and find answers to questions and problems, being able to do 20 things at once, reading this book and following my advice to **Build A Team, Educate Yourself, Have A Goal and TAKE ACTION!** Recognize it is a journey and not a race. Most importantly, "Never, never, never give up," -Winston Churchill. I look forward to meeting you and not being *"The Only Woman in The Room."*

Deborah Nye

First an investor, then an agent, Deborah Nye bought her first investment property in 2008. The property was a 2BR small row house that needed total renovation. After completing it pretty quickly with few problems, Deborah continued to purchase and renovate and worked her way up to large multi-unit buildings. She prides herself on developing relationships, giving back, and being a "decent" landlord.

Joining DIG, part of a national real estate investment association, in 2008, Deborah has been active in helping new investors achieve success. She has recently expanded her teaching to include Main Line School Night and other investing groups.

Deborah says, "I knew how to lay tile, paint, and scrape wallpaper by the time I was 13," having grown up with her dad renovating their houses while they lived in them. A graduate of Rhode Island School of Design, Nye continues, "I'm all those HGTV shows rolled into one, something my clients, friends and colleagues appreciate." Whether it be the layout and design of a property, or the financial aspects of a transaction, Deborah can "think way outside the box." She invests using the theory of "less properties higher yield" and will help you learn to "build a team, educate yourself, have a goal, and take action!"

Allow Your Why to Guide Strategy
by Gertrude Mageza

Your mind shines brightest when you enlighten others; your heart, when you
encourage others; your soul, when you elevate others; and your life,
when you empower others.
–Matshona Dhliwayo

Begin with your WHY. The desire to build wealth was the motivation that got me started in real estate I got here because I wanted to have more control of my destiny, I wanted to have financial freedom. I wanted to quit my job!!

Investing in real estate is not a get rich quick business. Therefore, it quickly became obvious that when things got tough, I needed something bigger than financial rewards, or quitting my job, to maintain my motivation.

You may not have the financial capability or the time to do what you want to do. Your why is not the mechanism of financial capability. You must have a WHY bigger than you as an individual. Identify your purpose in life, connect what you love to do to how you can make this world a better place for your family and your community.

Every business should have a clear strategy, a strategy that is a systematic plan to accomplish specific goals. A real estate business is no different, I applied the marketing skills of networking and risk-taking that I learned as a sales and marketing manager at British Airways to leverage my real estate business. The British Airways brand allowed me as a marketing manager to take bigger than usual risks to compete and maintain our leadership position in the marketplace, so my risk tolerance is a bit higher than most people.

As in marketing, there are always several strategies that can be deployed in real estate investing. These are your dreams: don't be afraid to use different budget scenarios or apply different creative approaches involving higher or lower perceived risks for your real estate business model. Not over-analyzing things and being able to take risks is a skill set I learned at British Airways that has helped me scale my real estate business. Figure out what your risk level is in real estate investing. On every deal you must establish risk and calculate the returns from your investment and compare that against not investing.

Of course, British Airways being an international super brand, one of the most important skills I learned there that I have transferred to my real estate business is the ability to build relationships with people from all walks of life. When you meet people, always find out how you can help the other person first, always seek to add more value than you take away. Be interesting and memorable to everyone you meet, develop strong ties that count so you can leverage their networks, as well as your own.

The First Steps

For me, my love for real estate crystalized as I was watching HGTV. I was inspired by the financial independence and success I saw on the screen. Individuals on the shows made it look fun and easy. A few hiccups here and there, but nothing too serious that ever derailed the projects, and *they always made money.* I wanted that too and I believed in my ability to make big money in real estate. I decided that I was not just going to be an HGTV fan, I would join them and reap the profits in real estate.

From there, I attended real estate trainings and Meetups. I read a lot of real estate books and joined Biggerpockets and other real estate-focused Facebook groups. I was not keen on spending a lot of money; reading and networking were better solutions for me. A great place to start your real estate journey is to join your local Real Estate Investor Association (REIA). My competence expanded from there. Even though you will not learn everything there, it is a supportive environment with very few sales pitches. Relationships are the key to success in this business. Not only can you learn from others' experiences, but these relationships may open additional opportunities. The bottom line, without networking you will not get far in this business. Your network in this business will eventually be tied to your net worth. I used to think that wealth was a prerequisite for real estate investment - I now know that *wealth is a byproduct of investment.*

The First Deal

At some point, I found myself in analysis paralysis. While I was confident I had a solid educational base, I now had to conquer the fear of starting a new venture and do a deal. My first step was to identify the strategy that helped me achieve my WHY the best. I landed on the core strategy to Buy, Rehab, Rent and Repeat. It is referred to as the BRRR strategy. Looking at this strategy, I had the connections that were required, and I had enough options to execute.

I searched the MLS and found a property that was bank-owned and abandoned. It was good I was a newbie - that limited my ability to go into too much detail about the property. I knew enough to work through the deal, but not enough to second guess myself. My offer was accepted, and I started my plan to rehab the property. It was a short rehab time, in fact, it was my fastest one to date. My only mistake was that I did not ensure all services were connected to the property. I was ready to get renters into the property and found out that the gas line to the property had been cut. An oversight quickly corrected, but it taught me to inspect properties more carefully, especially if they are bank-owned and had been unoccupied for a long period.

The first deal completed; I was more confident and was eager to get into the next deal. You can speak to your vision and strategy when invested. Commit to investing in your first real estate deal within three months. You will find that once you get started your progress accelerates. My stature within real estate investor social groups increased as well. As a woman investor, you can often be overlooked in networking settings. Groups of mainly men may not initially recognize the value of a woman, nor see them as a peer. Once they hear about your success, you quickly move from suspicious attendee to a respected font of knowledge.

Network Is Net Worth

Your reputation and networking skills have a direct impact when trying to acquire on and off-market properties. For on-market deals, brokers are often interested in your track record, what you have already closed. Off-market deals are heavily tied to your ability to network. Regardless of the method you use to purchase properties, relationship building is critical.

As relationships mature, you will start to get referral calls. Our best deal came through my husband's contact. They were attempting to get rid of an estate. The property totaled 24 units, duplexes and triplexes on the same street. This was a typical case of leveraging a relationship. Just like in marketing, develop an authentic personal brand that is consistent and easy for people in your network to remember. Intentionally network in the same direction of your long-term strategic goals – and your well-chosen relationships within that network will help you to achieve those goals. I believe we are always one contact away from our goal.

Before receiving that phone call, I focused on several key elements to help develop my network. First, I am always prepared to talk about what I do, and I am confident with my approach. Next, it is inevitable you will be asked, "What are you looking for?" Have more than a generic response about wanting a deal. Make sure your network understands what you do or what your business strategy is. Ask yourself, are the members in my network able to refer people and spread my message on my behalf? Last, I targeted people who could help us acquire the specific properties I sought. Having a long-term strategic plan for growing, developing and leveraging your network can yield massive results.

I prefer three or more units within a 50-mile radius from where I live. I wanted drivability to manage my properties. When the properties are within this radius, I can utilize the same renovation team. One of the greatest assets you have is your team, and networking to get the best team is a very important component of the overall process.

Renovation Team

I consider my process like an assembly production line. I schedule electrical, plumbing, painting, drywall, roofing on a rotating schedule when multiple properties are being developed. This process allows my contractors to have clear, consistent expectations, resulting in maximized profits. For example, they can buy bulk paint, as I use the same paint throughout all my properties. The easier the job is for my renovation team, the more money we all make.

Learning

Often, individuals will provide information that is helpful because they hope you will do the same. Listening to others provides the benefit of gaining knowledge from their experiences. Quite simply, it is a faster, more efficient way to learn information. Likewise, sharing information allows others to gain from your experiences. One concrete example of this is by sharing contacts. Sharing a contact provides a layer of confidence you might otherwise not have when hiring that resource.

Financial Discipline

My first deal gave me the confidence to engage investors in my vision. Using the same networking skills, I used for sourcing deals, I established good relationships with investors. My investors liked how my previous experiences revealed the importance of financial discipline and the importance of cash reserves.

Financial discipline is not only important for attracting investors, but also for operating a property. If you cannot responsibly handle money, you cannot make it in this business, as this business is primarily run on business debt. Tip: Before you get into this business, make sure you have your personal finances under control and are living way below your means. This is a good exercise in the same discipline needed to operate an investment.

Power of Leverage

Investors call leverage the eighth wonder of the world. If your investment property is appreciating, then the debt on an appreciating property is a good thing because of the leverage involved. Wise real estate investors reap the rewards of leverage but, remember, a prerequisite for this wisdom is financial discipline. High leverage alone will not make you rich in this business. It will certainly help you get started, but without the financial discipline to maintain adequate cash reserves, you may find yourself in a shortfall. Any experienced real estate investor will tell you that situations will arise that may literally and figuratively need you to fight fires and cash reserves will be the best fire extinguisher.

Growth and Scaling

Looking back, I see that the skills I used to scale originated from the skills I used to acquire my first duplex. At a very basic level, I knew that the more properties I owned, the more likely I could achieve my financial goals. From there, I focused on a city. Fortunately for me, the city I focused on was not popular with real estate investors (therefore, it was less competition). This area also interested me because a lot of infrastructure was planned for the immediate future. Due to the low competition, there were multiple multi-families on MLS at that time. Unfortunately, today, this is not the case (but on the flip side, it is good for me if I want to sell). While some may say it was a matter of luck, I believe it was my ability to recognize the opportunity in a market, and then finding the best deals within that market. This ties back to knowing what you want to invest in; I wanted to invest in cash-flowing properties that got me to financial freedom the fastest. Investing in this market did just that.

Creative financing is another important step I used to achieve my goal, specifically, for the 24-unit property. I ran the numbers from a variety of perspectives and analyzed the different outcomes. Ultimately, I chose a portfolio lender. For these types of transactions, you must produce a project plan in addition to the financial projections. For this project, I estimated 18 months to positive cash flow.

The last critical step in scaling using the BRRRR strategy is your loan selection. As BRRRR's third R stands for refinancing, it is important to position yourself in the most advantageous position to extract all the money you have invested, if not more. This directly ties to your ability to do the fourth "R," repeat. If your money is tied up on a property, it inhibits your ability to grow your portfolio. Regarding the refinance, most lenders only refinance up to 75 percent of the after-repair value. So, it is vital that the numbers work. You know the saying: "you make money when you buy the property," it is especially true with the BRRRR strategy.

Partners

As you grow and you do more deals or bigger deals choose your real estate partners very carefully. The best partners in this business will stand with you when things go wrong and will help identify solutions to steer the investment back on track to minimize losses. Choose partners based on their character first, and not their money. A complicated partnership agreement that involves lawyers cannot substitute a person's character and fairness. I am fortunate that the partnerships I have had have been with good people. The only mistake I made was to partner with a friend that had no real estate experience and they did not understand the risk factors when a deal did not go exactly as initially planned.

A lot of factors contributed to getting me where I am today. Ultimately, I was intentional about the lifestyle I wanted. That intention ties directly back to my WHY. Just like I did, I encourage you to start with your WHY. Then, visualize what you want your life to look like, and be specific. Determine what you want to do when your feet hit the ground in the morning. If you act and make sacrifices today, you will build the future you want.

Gertrude Mageza

Gertrude Mageza is originally from Southern Africa. She is the co-founder of Majestic Properties, a real estate investment company located in Boston, Massachusetts. A graduate of Northeastern University, with a strong sales and marketing background, she has used her business insight to help grow a multi-million-dollar family real estate investment business, that grew from two units to seventy units in twelve months. She is the host of the Real Estate InvestHer Meetup in Boston. Her passion is to see more women empowered and enter the real estate investor space so they can gain financial freedom and spend more time with their children.

Transitioning to an Entrepreneur
by Palak Shah

Our deepest fear is not that we are inadequate. Our deepest fear is that we are powerful beyond measure. It is our light, not our darkness that most frightens us. We ask ourselves, 'Who am I to be brilliant, gorgeous, talented, fabulous?' Actually, who are you not to be?
-Marianne Williamson

After my father passed away when I was very young, my mother – a teacher – pushed me to study and become a Mechanical Engineer. With little to no savings, she dreamed to see me in a steady full-time job. Climbing the corporate ladder is the gold standard for us middle-class folks. So, when I made it to a managerial position in an Engineering Department she was thrilled, and I was too – for having made her and my extended family proud.

As an Engineer, I worked for 17 years in corporate and took pride in being the only woman in the boardroom, paving the way for other women who wanted to do the same thing. As a woman in a male-dominated industry, one learns to constantly switch between two roles: the first one is being one of the guys and the second one is being the only woman around. After a while, I made that my normal and took pride in developing a thick skin. I loved my job, I traveled all over the world presenting a framework we had developed to increase the bottom line of factories that produced pharmaceutical glass.

And then in our late 30's, my husband and I decided to have kids. As a pregnant working mother, I took my cues from the images the media portrays. I wanted to be a jetsetter during the day and a nurturing mother in the evenings – because obviously (notice the sarcasm), infants only need parents at nights and working parents of young children do not need rest.

I thought I was making the financially responsible choice by waiting till my late 30's to have kids. The irony is, the higher up you go, the more demanding your job is, and the less time you have for your children. When the baby came, this ironic concept of "having it all" became clear to me. Even with two six-figure incomes, my husband and I found little remained after our monthly payments of sub-par childcare, mortgage and other conveniences we paid for to maintain two busy corporate lives and parenthood. Further, we did not have time for the baby. I left while the baby was sleeping and came back with bottles full of breastmilk, I had pumped throughout the day only in time to put her to bed. One day, as I was pumping breast milk in my office with newspapers covering the windows while on a conference call, I had a moment of clarity and I was filled with resentment. I felt like a lie had been sold to me for years.

Taking the Leap of Faith

A leap of faith must begin with a strong "why." For me, it was a clear need to be with my children. This need was way bigger than any formula, analysis or any convincing excel spreadsheet. It was even bigger than the embarrassment I expected if I failed at this endeavor and the shame I would feel within my professional circle being known as a mom who gave up on her career dreams. This need was VISCERAL. I believed in it with every fiber of my being. Taking the leap of faith began with the decision that my life could not continue the way it was. Something had to change. After much turmoil and months of strategizing, my husband and I decided it was time to become a single income family.

Formula for Becoming a Single Income Family

I decided to quit my job, but I still wanted to make an impact. We had purchased three rent-ready properties while I was still working. I knew real estate investing would be my path forward. I could see the impact it could have on wealth building and generating income for my family.

We sat down, crunched some numbers, and were able to use this formula to decide how many rental properties we would need to replicate my income.

Remember to use salary after taxes because depreciation offsets taxes after cash flow for most long-term rentals. One factor that played into it in my case was childcare expenses, which reduced dramatically when I quit my job, gas

and tolls (I drove about 100 miles per day for my job). Also consider 401k matching and other benefits, appreciation of properties, mortgage pay down by rent and some intangibles like the opportunity cost of your time being spent at a job as opposed to building a business for yourself.

After quitting my job, I immediately got to work, spending days with my children and late nights working on learning the new business. As I started working towards this, I ran into barriers that would stop me from scaling. I wanted to share those bottlenecks here because I believe every new investor must overcome these.

Barriers to Growing a Portfolio

Bottleneck 1: Capital

In becoming a single income family, even if I do not pay a single dime for childcare, we would not be left with enough money to grow and invest. Each time we wanted to purchase a property, we had to come up with a 25% down payment. Once we included closing costs and other expenses, in the market we were looking in, it was around $40,000 of seed money each time we purchased a property. That would limit our growth mainly because we would be limited by the amount of capital we could bring.

We read every book we could get our hands on, listened to hundreds of podcasts and got mentors and coaches to solve this problem. The strategy that came up repeatedly was BRRRR.

What is the BRRRR Strategy?

BRRRR is a value-add investing strategy which uses these steps:

Buy a distressed property below market value

Renovate it to increase its ARV (After Repair Value)

Rent it out – also known as stabilizing it

Refinance to a long-term mortgage pulling all your original cash out in the process and still cash-flowing

Repeat it, reinvesting the money to grow your portfolio

We knew that if we learned BRRRR and implemented it correctly, it would take away the capital constraints and it did.

Bottleneck 2: Construction Skills

Next, as I implemented this strategy, I realized I knew nothing about construction, nor buying distressed properties. I realized I needed to build my skill set to acquire and renovate properties – including construction budgeting, deal analysis and negotiating. I had used a contractor before for smaller projects and decided to stick with someone I trusted even if he was not the cheapest option out there.

If you are someone trying to gain construction skills, I highly recommend finding a reputable (and not necessarily the cheapest) contractor to do a project and spending as much time as you can at the job site, absorbing and learning.

Bottleneck 3: An Understanding of Finance

Another constraint I faced was not knowing enough about short and long-term financing. I called up banks, my mentors and other investors to see what the best way was to learn about finance. I spent weeks building relationships with banks and lenders to overcome this constraint.

Remember, there is no shortcut to this, and that "Fortune Favors the Finance Savvy!"

Bottleneck 4: Risk Taking Ability

There came a time when the education piece went as far as it could go. I knew that at some point, I had to take the risk and buy a distressed property for BRRRR. I used my skills as an engineer and a project manager to quantify risk. Quantitative risk management is converting the impact of risk on the project into numerical terms. This numerical information is frequently used to determine the cost and time contingencies of the project.

If you are struggling with risk-taking, here is something that can help. Say you are analyzing a BRRRR deal, and you are afraid your numbers are approximately $10,000 off. If your worst-case scenario becomes a reality, consider that $10,000 an investment in your education—you are unlikely to make the same mistake again.

Here are two personal examples:

I overpaid on my first investment property by $15K (I did not have a lot to invest at the time and it was a huge hit on my reserves), but eventually, I still built a multi-million-dollar, cash-flowing real estate portfolio. And guess what? I never made the same mistake again.

We had theft at another property because we didn't change the locks when we closed; my contractor was surprised how well I took it. No fingers were pointed, and no sleep was lost. It is all part of the business and built into the contingency. Lesson learned: I will change the locks on any property I acquire the very same day.

Final Bottleneck: Myself

During the first year, I purchased, renovated and refinanced five properties. And then, I realized that something was still shackling down the business and stopping the growth. **I found out that I was the bottleneck.** Because I was CEO, marketing, construction management, property management, bookkeeper and strategist for my company, the growth of my company was limited by the number of hours I could work on in a day myself. I applied all the strategies I had used to help other companies succeed at my previous job of 17 years to my current business. I built systems, teams and processes and leveraged them to remove myself as the bottleneck. Flash forward two years, the maintenance of my $4M portfolio I built in the past 2 years including growth i.e., deal analysis, acquiring more properties, managing construction work, finance, end to end property management and strategy only takes up three hours per day.

By the time I was done creating my $4 Million portfolio in two years, I had learned and implemented many strategies on:

- How to scale a business

- Using my corporate background to build and leverage systems, teams and processes
- Using my engineering side and love for numbers to get deal analysis and finance down to a science
- Dealing with the fear of failure and much more

Empowering Other Parents

When I reflected on the two years and the growth I had seen in the business, I wanted to shout from the rooftops the possibilities real estate investing can offer. This is especially true for families looking for the balance between building wealth for their family, and not missing out on the early years of their children. I started helping others to do the same. We launched a program to empower new investors with knowledge to build wealth and financial independence through Real Estate Investing. Teaching is a labor of love. As the daughter of a teacher, I know what good teachers can do in the lives of their students and the impact they can have on this world. My passion now is to help corporate parents get out of the stressful cycle through financial independence through the power of real estate investing.

Real Estate as a Way Out of the Two Choice Fallacy

There is a two-choice fallacy that us corporate folks are sold on – the two choices being 1. Be a corporate working parent and 2. Be a stay at home parent. I invite you to consider a third way, and that is entrepreneurship. Entrepreneurship gives us the freedom to get out of the cycle – because as an entrepreneur, you can make your own rules. Having a hidden advantage is limitless growth. Have you heard a business owner complaining about a ceiling? Never, because there just is not one! Entrepreneurship is limited only by the entrepreneur's vision and drive.

Spencer Johnson's question, "What would you do if you weren't afraid?" points to the core of what really stops us – fear. I want to propose a new way to mitigate that fear: this is a combination of the liberty that entrepreneurship provides and the low risk of passive income. Investing, especially in long term rental properties, is a low-risk strategy that allows you to pivot from the traditional career path and into the freedom of being able to spend more time on what is important to you: family, hobbies, philanthropy, fitness – the sky's the limit!

Palak Shah

Palak Shah is the founder and owner of Open Spaces Capital that generates over $1M in revenue. An Engineer by trade, after the birth of her two kids she made the move to entrepreneurship to be able to spend more time with her children. Though Palak has invested in real estate for many years, in her first two years investing full-time, she purchased, renovated, rented, and refinanced properties creating a $4M rental portfolio. It is now her passion to empower other investors to pursue entrepreneurship through real estate investing to live an empowered and financially free life through Open Spaces Women.

Channeling to Profits
by Rebecca Shea

*If you can't measure something, you can't understand it. If you can't
understand it, you can't control it. If you can't control it,
you can't improve it.*
– H. James Harrington

There are two types of people in the world who do marketing – the artists and the analysts. I learned this the hard way while looking to hire an assistant to take over my marketing. I sifted through tons and tons of applicants who wanted to sell me on their portfolio, how pretty they could make things, and how shiny this new object was. However, when I asked the question, "But does it work?" they looked at me like I was crazy.

"Well, marketing is a living thing," they would say.

"Everyone does it, so it OBVIOUSLY works," they would say.

"Of course, it will work! Haven't you heard of branding? This is the lifeblood of your business!"

Every one of these non-committal answers made my blood boil.

At this point, I was spending about $10,000 each month on marketing to feed my wholesaling business – by far, my biggest expense as a business owner – and I felt like there was no clarity on what would WORK. And it just did not seem like rocket science to me. (I should know, my husband is a full-blown rocket scientist.)

What I was looking for was a way to say, "If I spend this much money, the phone should ring this many times, we should get so many appointments, and if our sales team does their job, that will get us a certain amount of contracts." It seems like a common-sense way to run a business, right? Then why was it so hard?

I want to step back and talk about wholesaling – maybe clear up a few misconceptions - since I have sat on both the rehabber and the wholesaler side of the equation. First, some wholesalers are total sleazebags. It is true. And, so are some rehabbers. And, so are some policemen. And, so are some librarians…. You can find this with any profession. However, I like to believe a silent majority of people are good humans trying to do good things.

Second, wholesaling is a marketing and sales business. Rehabbing is a construction and project management business. Rentals are a strategist business and maybe the only true form of "investing." The problem is, most wholesalers are heavy on the "sales" side, and marketing is just a necessary evil to get them in front of that seller. Instead of trying to increase their net profit by getting more efficient with money spent on marketing, they default to their strength, sales. They throw more money into marketing to get more leads so they can increase their revenue, but this bloats their expenses without necessarily making the business healthier.

I did not start my wholesaling company by spending $10,000/month (or $20,000, which was what I was spending at the highest point). That journey started back in January 2016 when I joined a high-level real estate mastermind, 7 Figure Flipping (7FF). I was two and a half years into my investing journey and looking to scale from six rehabs per year to 12, so this seemed like the right place to be. Fixer Upper had aired a few seasons on HGTV and the joy that the hosts exhibited on each project was exactly how I felt inside. At that point, I *theoretically* knew about wholesaling, but not in a way that interested me. I was convinced that because I liked to make ugly things pretty, flipping is what I wanted to do for the rest of my life. It is funny how you never know where this journey will take you.

The other thing I did not realize was this "flipping" group was 80% wholesalers. (No worries, we fixed that. It's about 50/50 now.) But WOW were they awesome people! It was my first glimpse into the fact that wholesalers are not all creepy sleazebags looking for their Maserati. More importantly, what they were doing looked fun!

After a few months of getting exposed to the backend side of wholesaling, I decided to jump in and try it at a nominal level. Finding a house to rehab every month was eating up all my time and limited my ability to scale. If wholesaling provided me another revenue stream, all the better.

The first thing I did was ask to see behind the curtain of someone in the group who was wholesaling at a large scale so I could deconstruct the machine. In 2016 he did 186 wholesale deals in three markets and spent nearly $650,000 in marketing to make $1.9M gross revenue. He spent that money in eight "channels" (that's a fancy term for a method of marketing.) He made $2.85 for every dollar spent on marketing. That was his Return on Investment, or ROI. I know now this one ROI number tells me more than any other indicator regarding the health of a wholesaling business. That number will be important later. Hold on to it.

BUT WHAT ARE THE CHANNELS, BEKA? That is what everyone wants to know; it is the silver bullet answer. Heck, that is the thing I wanted to know when I started as well! Here is where I admit to some personal growth. I did not want to think that marketing was a living animal that has unique applications, but IT DOES! And I know this because I have analyzed 37 businesses, from wholesalers and rehabbers nationwide, who have spent over $5 million dollars in marketing in the past few years. Once other people realized that I had a knack for digging into the data and cutting out the fat, they threw their marketing information at me (I may have strong-armed a few too).

The data was very eye-opening. The surprising thing is how fluid it can be. A channel may work for six months, then stop working, and then it might work again two years later. Or, a channel might not work, but then you make a minor tweak, and it blows up. A wholesaler in California might be crushing it with Pay Per Click (PPC), while someone in North Carolina is getting abysmal results. The point is, as, with any journey, you must start somewhere. Take the first step. Then pay attention to what happens. Here is what I know from digging into dozens of businesses and millions of wholesaling marketing monies spent.

If you are looking to scale a wholesaling business, understand what it costs to get your phone to ring. For every call, only every third to fifth caller will be a qualified lead with a house to sell. The lead will want you to make an offer – to make an appointment, as soon as you can! Tracking this process will eventually show you to approximate how much it costs to get that appointment; for example, it could be $400. Now every single time you cancel an appointment or set an appointment so far out that the seller calls you to cancel because someone else got there first, just imagine lighting $400 on fire! That will motivate you!

The average marketing cost to get a contract at the time of writing this book is between $3000 to $5000. As the economy goes through its natural life cycles, this number will change. Tracking your numbers will give you advance indicators when this is happening.

And once that phone rings, your costs become irrevocably linked with how good your sales skills are – from answering the phone to the person sitting at the table with the seller. The lower end of these costs is in more rural markets with a lower assignment fee. Someone spending $3,000 to get a contract may be making $10,000 fees, while someone spending $5,000 to get a contract may be making $20,000 fees. That is why the ROI number, the $2.85 number I referenced above, is important.

If you are doing online marketing (PPC, SEO), nearly every webform submission will be a qualified lead. They have sought you out, not the other way around. The trick to converting them is speed – you **must** respond ASAP (within 5 minutes at the very most). If you are doing Facebook marketing, you will get a lot of tire kickers you have to wade through, but you can do that easily with a chatbot or a virtual assistant.

Even though there is no silver bullet, what I can give you are some overarching guidelines. First, ask yourself these three questions regarding your marketing objectives:

- Does it need to be scalable or are you looking for the lowest cost route for a few contracts?
- Do you live in a rural or urban area?
- Do you plan to put more *time* or *money* into your marketing?

The answers to those questions, dictate the channels you should implement (see the chart below I created to help you navigate your path).

TIME	MONEY	
Cold Calling **Texting**	**Pay Per Click (PPC)**	**URBAN**
Niche Lists Direct Mail **Door Knocking** **Door Hangers**	**SEO** **Facebook** **Equity List Direct Mail**	**RURAL** **&** **URBAN**
Bandit Signs **Driving for Dollars**	**Every Door Direct Mail**	**RURAL**

Pick one or two (at most) to start and go learn everything you can about them. Nearly everything I know about marketing I learned from the 7FF mastermind, but there are also podcasts, blogs and YouTube. I love we live in a time where people will give you step-by-step tutorials because they are proud of what they have learned and joyfully want to share it. This book is a perfect example of that.

After selecting your channel(s), track them! Set up a unique phone number for each channel, make sure all responses get put into a CRM or excel sheet, record how much money you spent and how much money you made with each one. That is where the fun begins, and where that $2.85 number becomes important.

If you are going to run a wholesaling operation at scale, target $3 made for every $1 spent on marketing (3:1 ROI), and here is why: In that scenario, your marketing is 1/3 of your profit. But your other overhead – namely people and systems – will be at least another 1/3. You want to make money, right?? If you track your channels and see one consistently returning you less than 2:1 ROI, cut it as it is costing you money to service that market. To be a super healthy company, shoot for 4:1 ROI!

I tracked my own stuff from day one, but I did not get laser-focused on dialing it in for a while. Once I did, I learned a few things. Namely, "that which gets measured, gets improved." By paying attention to these numbers, I could not only see which channels were not performing, but I could also identify what part of my wholesaling process was weak and needed improvement. The chart below shows my journey over an 18-month period.

Metric	Jan-Jun 2018	Jun-Dec 2018	Jan-Jun 2019
Call/Appt Ratio	2.8	3.4	3.4
Cost/Call	$142.40	$83.96	$67.74
Cost/Appt	$395.14	$288.93	$233.57
Cost/Closed Contract	$4,867.36	$3,619.24	$2,654.21
Profit/Closed Contract	$8,532.27	$10,460.95	$12,255.56
ROI	$1.75	$2.89	$4.62

In the past six years, I have rehabbed about 60 houses and wholesaled another 120. I have been a solopreneur, up to a team of nine people, and everywhere between. I have learned many, many lessons on this journey – some that have made me feel like I have conquered the world, some that have left me sobbing into a bowl of butternut squash soup. Even after I dialed in my marketing costs, I still struggled with scaling and maintaining a sales team. But, because I tracked my numbers, I knew exactly where the breakdown was. The sales team performance shows up in items like "canceled appointments" and "appointments to contract." And this too is part of the journey.

I never set out to be a wholesaler – I just wanted to make houses pretty. But without going down that road, I would not have discovered the language of marketing efficiency. The marketing consulting company I now run, MarketShark, has been directly responsible for businesses dramatically increasing their ROI. Using a real-life case study - one client spent $174,000 on marketing last year, and because of the consistent feedback loop on their performance, they improved their ROI by $0.81. Time after time, I have seen small changes yield huge results. Here, the small steps led to an additional $141,000 in revenue! That is powerful.

They say that the journey of a thousand miles starts with the first step. For those looking to get into marketing, that first step is realizing there is no silver bullet - pick a channel and do it. However, if you want a smoother path for your journey, the second, third and fourth steps are to measure, understand and improve upon that marketing!

Rebecca "Beka" Shea

Over the past 6 years, Beka Shea has rehabbed over 60 houses and wholesaled over 120 deals. Prior to launching her real estate journey, she served as an officer in the US Navy, and then spent 7 years working as a mechanical engineer in the energy efficiency arena. After her third daughter was born, she decided to hang up her traveling hat and focus on real estate investing. Her wholesaling journey started as a path for ensuring a steady supply of properties to feed the rehab machine. After much trial and error in the marketing world, she applied her engineering skills to improving ROI by relentlessly evaluating business marketing with real time feedback. In the process, she consulted with other high-level investors and launched an elite marketing consulting business, MarketShark. Her passion for efficiency and helping others succeed poured out into her investing mastermind, where she spent the past 3 years leading small group accountability sessions for hundreds of other investors

Today Beka works full-time with the real estate investing mastermind, 7 Figure Flipping, heading up Membership Development, while also providing marketing consulting for some of the nation's top wholesaling operations.

Construction Management Tools
by Andresa Guidelli

I raise up my voice—not so that I can shout, but so that those
without a voice can be heard.
-Malaya Yousafzai

Born and raised in Brazil, I grew up with parents who supported my wildest ambitions with the guidance and the assurance that, if needed, I could always come back home. At 14 years old, I asked if I could move out. Yes, you heard me right, my age was not a typo. I asked them if I could live in another town, go to a tech school during the day and take English classes at night. They agreed to my proposal. This experience, among many others, not only instilled confidence in me, but also prepared me to lead construction teams and inspire other women to live financially free and balanced lives through real estate.

After college, I decided to come to the US for an exchange cultural program and six months later, I was approved to start my master's degree. I did not know a single person when I moved to the US and I had no clue how I would be able to pay for my degree, but that did not stop me. I built relationships that gave me the support I needed, and I found work, sometimes two jobs and on weekends, to pay for everything. Of all the jobs I did, the hardest one was door to door sales; however, it proved to be the most rewarding. It taught me to have thick skin and provided real-world experience I could not gain in the classroom.

Here is the reason I am telling you all this information about my personal journey. I was not born in the US. English is not my first language. I indeed have an accent and for sure make grammar mistakes all the time! I did not have the funds to pay for college nor my master's degree. And, I had no clue what real estate even was, nor construction management! So, before you continue reading this chapter, let's leave all the excuses at the door; about why you cannot build your wealth. Embrace that we are where we are supposed to be, and it is on us to step forward and have a seat at the table.

Before you start reading this, I want you to know one thing: **You do not need to know everything about construction to manage a project.** Richard Branson, business magnate, was asked what made him so wealthy, "Surround yourself with people that are smarter than you and your business will thrive." With this perspective in mind, I will go over a few strategies that will propel you to make the "right" decisions while building a team around you to support and implement your wildest dreams.

Size Matters

The size of your construction project will determine the level of management skills required to run it efficiently. It will also dictate the tools and systems you need to implement to be able to scale your business without losing your mind. Your job, as an investor, is to implement your vision by hiring the "right" people for the "right" seat (I highly recommend you read the book *Traction* by x). Can a handyman build a new construction project? Probably yes, however, it would take much less time if you hire a general contractor (GC) who has several crews. Can a GC do minor repairs on my rental located on a C- or B+ neighborhood? Yes, however, it is probably cheaper to have a handyman execute smaller jobs.

In real estate, it is important to match the project type with the professional's skill level. I get asked all the time if I can recommend a GC and my answer is always the same: "It depends. What type of project is it?" A rental grade project usually takes two to five handymen to do the job in a couple of weeks. Materials are usually funded by the owner and invoice requests are often processed through text messages. I might be oversimplifying things intending to emphasize there is nothing wrong with not using sophisticated software to manage the project; simple processes can also be successful. If you are looking to manage a project that requires minor repairs, I would recommend a few things:

- If you are buying the material, order everything on-line and request your GC to pick it up. Make sure the material is indeed being used at your project. Save all your materials list so you do not need to build that again on your next project.
- Print the layouts and tape them on the walls. It is important for the crew to have a visual (for example, a tile layout).

You should communicate in their native language so there is no miscommunication. Believe me, they will nod their head as confirmation they understand what you are saying, where, sometimes they are ashamed to admit they did not understand you. I have found three ways to resolve this problem. Learn their language. It is difficult to learn another language, but I will still encourage you to do it. Have fun! Translate all documents into their language. When you are face-to-face, download a translator and make sure any text messages you send are written in their native language.

For full gut projects, I expect the GC to have a crew and sub out major trades such as electric, plumbing and HVAC. I also look for someone who can do a few properties simultaneously and can communicate through technology, eliminating the need to meet in-person daily. Here are my recommendations:

- Even if your GC says he/she can handle multiple projects at the same time. Start with one to see how the entire project goes before awarding several projects to the same GC.
- Do not micro-manage. Walk the project at least once a week (depending on size, the frequency might vary).
- Have all documents for a project saved in a Dropbox folder named with the street address. Include the following sub-folders:

  - Closing Buying
  - Closing Selling / Refi
  - Lender
  - Architect
  - General Contractor
  - Legal docs / Taxes
  - Private Lenders
  - Pictures

For new construction projects, I look for a more sophisticated GC who works directly with a Project Manager that will facilitate the communication between us and move the project along. Due to the size of the project, GC must use a software program and have significant experience building multiple properties at the same time. Here is a list of additional expectations:

- GC runs the company as a business and does not need payment to get started on the next construction phase.
- GCs who handle large scale new construction projects typically install "builder's grade" finishes. If this is not what you want, be clear from the beginning.
- With new construction, there are typically very few change orders. Pre-construction planning is very important and will determine how successful your new construction project will be.

Good GCs Only

"My GC did not show up at the project today," or "My GC walked away with my money," are the two of the most common phrases I hear from women. Before I share tips on how to avoid those situations, I want to say three things: No GC comes with guarantees, it is your fault if the project goes over budget or overschedule, and it is typically your fault if the project does not provide the returns you were expecting. However, thoroughly vetting a GC can potentially save you money, time and tears.

Here are my recommendations:

- Meet them at their job site first.
- Arrive 10 to 15 minutes early. My time is valuable, and I recognize other people's time is too. If he/she is late and did not give me a heads up by text or call, this is a deal-breaker for me. I believe if someone is a bad communicator from the start, that is a good indicator he/she will behave like this during the project. Remember, this is one my non-negotiables and you might adjust accordingly to what works for you.
- Schedule this meeting mid-morning or mid-afternoon. This will show how their crew works; if there is nobody working, I do not hesitate to ask where they are.

- Ask a lot of questions about the project itself and his/her business. Also, observe the look of the project. You can tell a lot about the operations of a business by examining the cleanliness of the site, the number of people working, if permits are displayed and fences are in place.
- Observe the communication between the GC and the crew. Respectful conversations create positive energy and that is a must:
  - Review their contract with a fine-tooth comb
  - Was the quote delivered in time?
  - Is there a cost breakdown, or just a lump sum?
  - Is the document well organized?
- Walkthrough of your project:
  - Did he/she take notes, pictures and measurements?
  - Can he/she work with communication apps and software such as Slack,
  - Dropbox, or Google Drive?
    - Is he/she asking you lots of questions to understand how you can work better together?

Following these recommendations will either show you red flags or the right GC for your project.

Mind Your Own Business

It would be a wonderful day if all GC's run their construction practices as a business. Typically, if a GC needs a large deposit to get started or he/she needs you to fund the construction cost, upfront, prior to the next phase, it is normally a sign he/she does not have enough capital to run his/her own business. There are three options when you encounter this situation:

1. Find someone else.

2. Work with them but know you will need to upfront all costs.
3. Work with them but renegotiate so you only pay for work completed.

While some GCs operate by a handshake, you must require a contract (blame it on your company's policies, even if you are the only person in your company). Do not, I repeat, DO NOT write a check before you have a contract in place. Here are a few additional tips prior to writing your first check:

Give:

- A Scope of work: including a detailed description of what needs to be done
- A Finishes' list: list of all the finishes you would like to use (model + price + link + pic)
- Your own contract revised by YOUR attorney

Get:

- Copy of their updated license - This shows he/she indeed has one and it is current
- W9. A 1099 is required to be sent to each contractor at the end of the project, and a W9 is needed to issue the 1099
- Signed contract with the following addenda:

  - Scheduling
  - Payment plan

Everything Is Negotiable

I negotiate regardless of the estimate. For me, it is as simple as brushing my teeth every day; I brush it regardless of if I ate or not. It is just part of the process. I have found that the more I negotiate, the more comfortable I feel with negotiating. I was not comfortable with negotiating when I started, but here is how I built my skill and confidence:

By working with so many men, I learned that they negotiate all the time and they expect others to negotiate.

I can negotiate confidently without being forceful, disrespectful or making the other party feeling undervalued. It is all about having negotiation tactics.

I read the book *Never Split the Difference* (this is a must) and implemented a lot of tips I learned from this book. Those lessons have allowed me to negotiate with every single trade and saved several zeros off the total, without compromising the quality or relationship with the vendor.

I do not expect to have a home run in every single negotiation. There are projects with bigger margins than order and it needs to be considered.

The biggest thing for me is to build a solid relationship that will last longer, so I make sure I take care of people.

Regardless of whether you agree with all the recommendations I have given, I ask you to give all of them a try. If something does not work, adjust accordingly. Building standard practices create clear expectations, and expectations give an opportunity for people to deliver high-quality services.

The success of your business is directly related to how often you are using your toolbox. As you grow, you will need new tools to build the company and live the lifestyle you want. Those tools will allow you to claim your seat at tables where the decisions are made, and new opportunities are created. Some of those tables might not fit your vision so I encourage you to build your own table and invite others from your community with the same values and goals to join. All the women in this book are behind you.

Andresa Guidelli

Andresa was born and raised in Brazil. She is Lorenzo's mother, Women's Rights advocate and a developer who specializes in full gut renovation projects, new construction and is focusing on building medium to larger commercial developments. She owns a rental portfolio, comprising both long and short-term rentals.

Andresa also runs a mastermind called "LeadHers in Construction - Women Who Build Together", where a group of women, who are also passionate about construction, gather on a monthly basis to mastermind around goals and challenges they face at their job sites. The goal is to provide clear actions steps and accountability to make the construction process less stressful and more productive.

Andresa is the co-founder of The Real Estate InvestHER® Community, a platform to empower women to live a financially free and balanced life through both in-person meetings across the US and Canada and an on-line membership that offers accountability and mentorship for women to take their business to the next level on their own terms. She is also the co-host of the "The Real Estate InvestHER Show," a podcast providing straight talk strategies with inspiration from successful women who share their journey.

On her personal side, she loves dancing salsa and practicing water painting during her free time.

www.therealestateinvesther.com

@therealestateinvesther

Strategic Moments to Build an Empire
By Liz Faircloth

Understand that the right to choose your own path is a sacred privilege. Use it. Dwell in the possibility.
-Oprah Winfrey

As the saying goes by Lao Tzu, *A journey of a thousand miles begins with one single step.* Although this saying is overused, it is so true. That is exactly how I started my journey of real estate investing back in 2004, 16 years ago.

I will not bore you with every detail of these last 16 years, but I will share six strategic moments along my journey that have helped me build my business. As I share these strategic moments, I have added learned lessons and *calls to action* so you can leave this chapter with action steps for yourself, not just a bunch of inspiration you cannot do anything with!

First Strategic Moment – Observe the Masses and Do the Opposite

I went to college at Rowan University, where I majored in psychology. I was very driven in college (to put it nicely) and my goal was to open my own counseling practice. To achieve this goal, I planned on getting my master's degree in Social Work (MSW) and then a Doctorate in Psychology. I was accepted into The University of Pennsylvania for my master's and I was on my way to fulfilling my professional dream. During graduate school, a few strategic moments happened that changed the trajectory of my future forever.

My brother in law, Tony, was the first entrepreneur I knew. After college, he pursued his dream of running an organization to empower college students. I was fascinated that he was living his life on his terms. During my first year in graduate school, he gave me a book called *Rich Dad Poor Dad* by Robert Kiyosaki. My life was forever changed because of reading this book. Like many other investors, *Rich Dad Poor Dad* opened my eyes to so many concepts I was not familiar with – passive income, financial independence and the power of real estate investing. I came from a middle-class family and parents that taught me the importance of work ethic, integrity and passion. The whole idea of having money "work for me" was new and I really was intrigued by this idea.

Rich Dad Poor Dad got my wheels turning about business, entrepreneurship and real estate investing. Since I was taking classes at the University of Pennsylvania for my graduate degree in Social Work, I got the idea to take a class on entrepreneurship at the Wharton School of Business. This was unheard of …. a graduate student in one school wanting to take classes in a completely different school. However, my parents taught me early on to "Observe the Masses and Do the Opposite." So, I went to my school advisor and I had to jump through a bunch of hoops to take a class at the Wharton School, but I was committed to making it happen and they finally allowed me to enroll in the class. This class was a game-changer for me. As a class project, I created a business plan to launch a counseling firm focused on serving …. yes, you guessed it …. women. I loved what I was learning there more than what I was learning from my graduate degree classes and I wanted to explore more with entrepreneurship and real estate investing but, I was not sure how to do this

As graduation from Penn quickly approached, I made a hard, but important decision. I decided to not pursue a path in social work, but instead in business. I wanted to learn how to sell and how to build a business and I was very intentional that I wanted to work for a *woman* entrepreneur. Fortunately, I found that: a small consulting company in New Jersey, led by a wonderful woman entrepreneur. She taught me a ton about business, entrepreneurship, sales and people. I worked at this company for 10 years and will be forever grateful for that experience.

Strategic Call to Action – Observe the masses and do the opposite. Be open to all possibilities, even if the masses are moving in a different direction than you are. That is probably a sign you are up to something amazing. Listen to your heart and follow the inspiration around you. Look at what you are doing today (how you are spending your time) and then evaluate what you are doing today whether it is helping or hindering you from achieving your long-term goals and aspirations. Use yourself as the measuring stick, not other people.

Second Strategic Moment – Get the First Deal Done by Finding Tired Landlords

One of the dangers in this business is taking too long to get your first deal done. Yes, you want to make the right decisions and not just get into *any* deal, however, at some point after you educate yourself, you must take the plunge and get your first deal done.

My First Deal

During my last month of graduate school, I met my now-husband Matt through our best friends (Amanda and Rick) who were brother and sister. At first, I did not like him (sorry, Matt!), but through his persistence and our common love for red wine, I finally came around. We had an amazing first date talking about our goals and what we want out of life. This was not the typical first date, so I knew I met someone special. I gave him *Rich Dad Poor Dad* to read and we played Robert Kiyosaki's CashFlow game on one of our first dates. He was hooked just like me. Together we took the plunge and made a goal that within a year we would buy our first rental property.

Our first step was to get educated since we knew nothing about investing. We attended at least a year of courses and workshops through Philadelphia's Diversified Investor Group Organization. We found our first deal by trying to find "tired landlords" through calling them via newspaper "For Rent" ads. The philosophy with calling "For Rent" ads is that if the landlord is marketing their vacancy, then they might be frustrated that they have a vacancy, and therefore, might be motivated to sell. Most investors today do not realize how many of these smaller multifamily properties are owned by individual investors, like the one that became our first investment; a duplex. According to the U.S. Census Bureau's 2015 Rental Housing Finance Survey, individual investors made up the largest percentage of the housing market. Individual investors account for 74.4% of rental properties. As you search for small multifamily opportunities, the chances are very high you will be dealing with one of these individuals. Further, there is a strong possibility these individual investors have owned their properties for quite some time and could be very motivated to sell.

Back to our first deal. This calling "For Rent" ads strategy worked for us after about 100 cold calls. We found a young guy who worked full-time and did not want to be a landlord anymore. He owned a duplex in the Roxborough section of Philadelphia. We learned a lot with this deal, and this began our appreciation for multifamily. The biggest lesson for us was the importance of onboarding your new tenants. We did not realize these tenants are so (I mean so!) used to their previous landlord's rules and expectations. Within a month of owning this duplex, one tenant moved out and we had to evict the other tenant. This is quite common when you take over a property. However, allowed us to renovate the units and onboard tenants that met *our* criteria.

Strategic Call to Action– Move through your fear and do whatever it takes to get your first deal done and behind you. Learn and grow through any mistakes you make and then apply these learnings to the next deal. Create a plan that includes multiple ways to get in front of "tired landlords" who are motivated to sell and are fed up with being a landlord in your target market area. Lastly, always have a transition and onboarding plan with your new tenants.

Third Strategic Moment – Live Below Your Means

After holding the duplex in Philadelphia for about a year, we moved to New Jersey to begin our married life together. After a couple of years of owning our first deal, the duplex, we decided to do a 1031 exchange into a four-unit in New Jersey. We wanted to focus on growing our real estate portfolio closer to home. During this same period, we decided that it was the right time for Matt to quit his job to focus full-time on real estate. When we were looking for our house, we bought a house with a mortgage I could handle on my own (without my husband making a dime). This was a very strategic move for us as it allowed us to reinvest the money made from real estate, back into the business. Like most new businesses, the first few years we made money, and we lost money. However, the personal sacrifice to buy a smaller house, with cheaper expenses, ultimately allowed us to grow our business into what it is today.

When Matt quit his high paying job, we were not collecting enough rental income to support us financially. We took the leap of faith and decided to figure it out. By no means am I saying I would recommend this to everyone. Honestly, we were in our 20's and a bit naive. I speak with a lot of investors, at all stages of their life and they cannot take the same risk we took. The great thing about real estate investing is you do not have to copy my journey to find success on your own. Regardless of your personal situation, the key to getting started on this path is by first, getting your financial house in order; one strategy to get you there is to live below your means.

Additional Strategies:

Have you created both a personal and business budget? Do you stick to it and review it consistently?

Are you tracking and monitoring your spending and looking for ways to cut out meaningless spending?

Are you setting yourself up to take advantage of "good" debt?

Do you have a plan in place to eliminate "bad" debt?

How can you downsize your home/living situation?

Strategic Call to Action — Take some time to answer the above questions. And then decide on three ways in the next 30 days YOU are going to "live below your means."

Fourth Strategic Moment – Focus, Focus, Focus

As I mentioned, Matt and I were very naïve when we began our real estate investing journey. I wish we had more mentors and better direction. We got involved with so many types of projects – way too early. In the first three years of business, we bought single-family houses, bought raw land to develop, bought a commercial building and bought rentals. I would not suggest anyone to repeat what we did. Our path is our path. We learned a lot from our experiences, and it is the reason we are where we are today, I am grateful for it.

Although I am thankful for our journey, one of the biggest lessons I have learned along the way is there is SO MUCH power in focus. Depending on who you are and your own personality, this will be easy for some and extremely difficult for others. While I think it is valuable to learn about different niches in real estate investing, I also have seen the power of scaling your portfolio (sooner than later) when you focus and "go all-in" on an area.

In 2010, right when we began raising private money to fund our multifamily deals, we focused on multifamily. The reason you want to focus is to leverage your knowledge, time and energy towards one area. You cannot be the master at everything in this business. Some of the most amazingly successful investors I have met over the years got there because they focused. This is not as exciting and sexy, but if you want to build a scalable business there is no greater power than focusing on one niche. Each time you begin your next project, you take what you learned from the previous project and apply it to have a more efficient process and project.

When we purchased a 50-unit building, our largest acquisition at the time was an 18 unit. This growth was possible because we focused solely on apartments. This purchase also aligned with our goals and we were applied all the lessons we learned from the smaller projects to this new one.

Strategic Call to Action – Find your niche, became a master at it – do it repeatedly. Focus your time, money and energy towards it. If you are not confident that you have found the niche you want to "go all-in" on, then interview at least two people in the niches you are interested in and learn everything you can about their experience.

Fifth Strategic Moment – Know When to Expand Past Your Comfort Zone

For about 10 years, we had a rule we bought nothing over 30 minutes from home base. We had a local team under our umbrella that managed everything for us. When we landed the 50-unit deal, an hour and a half away from our home, we realized our team could not manage this building and we had to hire our first 3rd party property management team.

We had to let go of directly managing and instead shift to being an asset manager. It was very helpful in this scenario we had a local partner 10 minutes from the property. It is always helpful to have someone on the ownership side (or employed by the owner) that is local to the building and that can be the local feet on the ground. Yes, the property manager will be local, but you (the owner) also want to be locally represented.

Acquiring this property opened our eyes to expanding markets and creative financing strategies. Since this acquisition, we primarily focused on buying properties out of state with most of our acquisitions in the past two years being outside our local area.

A few key lessons learned on the 50 unit:

- It might benefit you to have the property management company, who will manage the property, become a passive investor in the project. That way, they have skin in the game and financially benefit from the strong performance of the asset as an investor.
- Create and stick to a process to manage the property manager (which in larger multifamily is called asset management). Remember, this third-party manager has various owners who they work with, so you must establish with them what type of communication and updates you require. It is all about managing them to the business plan that has been established.
- This was our seventh syndication and was our largest raise at that point. We raised over $1 million, which included 17 investors. One thing we learned on this deal was that investors will back out and change their mind at the eleventh hour. You want to account for this and plan ahead. Always have more options on private money sources than you need to close.
- When you purchase these types of deals, assume a stabilization period will be needed, regardless of the sellers' reported occupancy numbers. Unlike single-family, apartment owners are not required to disclose everything about a property. No matter how much due diligence you do before closing, there are always things you learn after closing.
- Maintenance costs – the larger the property, the more important it becomes to leverage the time and cost of your maintenance team. Designate specific days for your staff to visit the property and

knock out all the issues. This will reduce your overall expenses.

Strategic Call to Action – If you seriously are considering investing out of state, learn as much as you can about this strategy and build a team in advance. You cannot buy a property in another state without a solid process and a solid team. Both will be critical to your success.

Sixth Strategic Moment – Launching The Real Estate Investher® Movement

When I had my first child in 2013, I decided it was time to leave my corporate job and begin a new chapter in my life. I wanted to focus my energy on my soon to be child (since we waited a long time to have kids) and on our real estate investing business.

Right around 2015, I met Andresa Guidelli. I first met her on BiggerPockets, and we immediately hit it off when we met in person for coffee. Over the next several years, we became good friends and had a shared love for empowering women. During 2015, we launched a women-focused mastermind group that met once a month via Skype (which is still running today.) We also partnered on flips and new construction projects. Over our many coffee meetings, we would chat about our young kids, balancing it all as moms and wives, our real estate business and everything in between.

We talked about our shared passion for supporting and empowering women (in particular) in this business. We got increasingly frustrated when we would attend real estate investing meetups and conferences we would be the only woman speaking. We wanted to be part of a community that lifted each other up in the space of investing, finance, financial freedom and wealth building. Unfortunately, we could not find such a community. So, like most entrepreneurs, we created our own.

With tons of passion, enthusiasm and a mission to support women living a financially free and balanced life, we launched our podcast, the Real Estate InvestHER® Show. Early on, I had a smart guy tell me I would eventually "run out of women" to interview. I just smiled when he said this. His comment gave me the extra motivation to continue to find the exceptionally brilliant women I have the pleasure of interviewing

Fast forward two years later, we have an amazing and committed tribe of women called "InvestHERs." Our mission is to build an online and in-person community to support tens of thousands of women around the globe to live a financially free and balanced life on their own terms. It has been so inspiring for us to witness so many women in our community find their inner confidence, take action and buy their first or next investment property - all from the support of women cheering them on, providing real support and collaborating together rather than competing against one another.

Strategic Call to Action – When you make your why bigger than you, amazing things happen. All my professional experience for the last 20 years led me to the Real Estate InvestHER®. Now you need to look inside of you. What is your passion? What do you stand for? What can you create that is bigger than you?

Liz Faircloth

Liz Faircloth co-founded the DeRosa Group in 2005 with her husband, Matt. The DeRosa Group, based inTrenton, NJ, is an owner of commercial and residential property with a mission to "transform lives through real estate. "DeRosa has vast experience in bringing properties to their highest and best use, which includes repositioning single-family homes, multi-family, apartment buildings, mixed-use, retail, and office space. The company controls close to 700 units of residential and commercial assets throughout the east coast.

Liz is super passionate about her work with the Real Estate InvestHER® Community. Liz is the co-founder of The Real Estate InvestHER® Community, a platform to empower women to live a financially free and balanced life through both in-person meetings across the US and Canada and an on-line membership that offers accountability and mentorship for women to take their business to the next level on their own terms. She is also the co-host of the "The Real Estate InvestHER Show," a podcast providing straight talk strategies with inspiration from successful women who share their journey.

Liz has been interviewed for many articles and top-rated podcasts, including being a two-time guest on the top-rated BiggerPockets Podcast and the Best Ever Show. On the personal side, Liz is an avid runner,has completed several triathlons and marathons, has two adorable children and is a New York Mets Fan.

DeRosa Group Website: www.derosagroup.com

The Real Estate InvestHER Podcast: www.therealestateinvesther.com

The Fruit of Consistent Hard Work
By Rebecca Rynkiewicz

Luck is what happens when preparation meets opportunity.
–Seneca

In 2014, recently divorced, broke and $80,000 in credit card debt, I moved back to my hometown of Doylestown, PA. I had been selling real estate for two years in Columbus, Ohio, and left my clients to start my life and career over in Pennsylvania. I was stressed, depressed and felt like I would never be able to survive on my own. All I could afford was a 1940s, 900 square foot Cape Cod rental in the country suburbs of Philadelphia, with my English Bulldog, Charley. Sitting on my living room floor one evening shortly after moving in, surrounded with boxes to be unpacked and a glass of red wine in hand, I was reflecting on my life and asking myself, how did I get here?

I knew exactly how; I built my life around my ex-husband and made all my decisions based on him. I was living a life by default, and not by design. On the surface I looked happy, but deep down I was miserable. When I found out he was having multiple affairs, it was the wakeup call I needed to make a big change. I deserved better than this.

Sitting on the living room floor that day, I had an epiphany. I read the book *Think and Grow Rich* by Napoleon Hill. When Napoleon said, "Whatever the mind of man can conceive and believe, it can achieve, through a positive mental attitude," I knew he was speaking directly to me. I decided to flip the "woe is me" mindset and turn my negatives into positives by turning my obstacles into opportunities. After all, I had my real estate license since 2012 and had a relatively successful career in the last two years selling in Columbus, Ohio. There was no reason I could not accomplish the same success, or more, in my hometown. I would not let my failed marriage and the life I lead in my 20's define me. I was destined for much more than this. I was turning 30 and starting my life over. I quickly got my real estate license in PA and got to work.

The Steps

Returning to my hometown, after being away for over ten years, was challenging. Specifically, building a relationship-based business when you do not know anyone, market saturation with more experienced realtors who had a stronghold on certain neighborhoods, and my lack of familiarity with the area all posed initial obstacles I needed to overcome. However, I didn't let that stop me.

I made a game plan on how I would attack every single day of my new life on the road to reinventing myself. I followed 3 simple steps:

- Establish my PMA: Positive Mental Attitude.
- Create my Plan of Action: I found an agent in my brokerage firm to model myself after, and created the same daily rituals and habits they had and implemented them into my day
- Begin every day with the end in mind

The Implementation

I showed up to my Brokerage daily. I asked to shadow the top 5% of agents in the office doing most of the business. I found the single top producing realtor in my office, who at the time was selling around $10,000,000 in volume annually. I saw what she did daily, weekly, monthly, to get her to where she was. I wrote down a goal in my home office: $10,000,000 in closed volume annually. I had no idea how I would get there. Looking back now, that number seemed so incredibly daunting to me. I would have to sell over 40 houses a year to get to this number, and I had no leads, nor, no sphere of influence to get started.

I asked every agent in my office that had listings in a first-time homebuyer price point to hold open houses for their listings. Most agents do not like doing open houses so they happily obliged. I did at least one open house a week. I made sure I marketed these open houses to the best of my ability. I put out directional signage hours before the open. I made up property flyers, partnered with a lender to give payment estimates on the house, and distributed them by knocking on every door in the neighborhood. I also blasted it on every social media platform. My open house turnouts were great! I used sign-in sheets to capture buyer (and sometimes seller) lead info and immediately went home and put them into a CRM system and created drip campaigns. Finally, I executed the most important step; I diligently followed up with **every single lead**.

When I was not doing open houses, I was door-knocking certain neighborhoods in areas I chose to farm. I did this at least twice a week. I also got a lender to share the cost of purchasing Zillow leads in the zip code I lived in. My budget was a hefty $300/month- which at the time was every spare penny I had.

For almost six months, I did not see any type of result. I grinded every day, handwriting personal notes to people I met at networking events, open houses and during my door-knocking efforts. I posted on social media. I made phone calls daily. I called my immediate and extended family members and asked them for referrals. As soon as I received a lead through Zillow, I called them right away. The typical responses were: "Sorry, we just are not ready to buy," "We don't think the market is strong enough and we will not get what we want if we were to sell now," "We decided to go with another agent who has more of a presence in our neighborhood" and "Call back in six months, we may be ready then." I was not getting anywhere. When I was feeling defeated, after putting in 50-60 hours a week of work with no result (or money coming in may I add), it is tough to be positive. Despite all of this, I kept my PMA! I trusted the process. Ultimately, I got a part-time job waitressing to pay the bills. Times were certainly tough.

The Results

This time in my life taught me a lot about patience. It truly is one of the most important things to embrace in life. You can put tremendous energy into something, and not see immediate results. This is called the Plateau of Latent Potential: Habits and efforts often appear to make no difference until you cross a critical threshold and unlock a new level of performance. Everyone's critical threshold is different. Think about a fruit tree, what is the last thing to grow on the tree? First, the seed must germinate. Then the roots grow. Next, you see it sprout and then the trunk grows big and strong. You will then see the branches grow. Leaves will bloom. Finally, one day, the fruit appears, and it is the most delicious thing you have ever tasted!

My real estate career is comparable to this fruit tree. One day, it was like everything clicked. I received a phone call from a seller I had been calling, mailing and texting for months, letting me know they were ready to list their house with me. A few days later, a buyer that met me at an open house had let me know they were ready to buy and asked me to put them in touch with a lender to get pre-approved. It felt as though almost every week, I received a call or email like this. Before I knew it, I was closing at least one to two deals a month, all while still putting forth the effort that got me to this place. My clients were then giving me referrals for their friends and family, and soon my database was growing rapidly. By the end of 2015, I had closed 26 transactions and $3,500,000 in volume. It was nowhere near my goal of $10,000,000 I had established at the beginning of the year, but it was a far cry from having no business at all.

I kept the momentum going into 2016 and was introduced through my brother to three friends who started a home-flipping business. They were interviewing realtors to help them buy and sell their finished product and they chose me after interviewing a bunch of agents. I learned through these three guys what to do, and, more importantly, what *not* to do, with house flipping. I worked closely with them, helping them buy, sell and pick finishes for seven different homes over the course of two years. I knew I wanted to get into flipping, but never felt fully "ready."

If I learned anything since my divorce, it was that you are never ready for anything in your life! So many people are always "getting ready to get ready." US entrepreneurs jump off the cliff and build the parachute on the way down. That is what I did - I purchased my first flip in May 2018, with my Dad, with cash I saved from real estate commissions ($83,500) and put $110,000 into the rehab. Half of the rehab funds were borrowed from a friend who lent us private money, and the other half I put on credit cards and used commissions as they rolled in from real estate sales. When it was all said and done, I sold the house for $332,000, I walked away with a net profit of over $117,000! It was quite the learning experience. There are many things I would do differently moving forward, including vetting contractors better, not paying them in full for work yet to be completed (rookie mistake). In the end, it was the best way to learn how to be a successful flipper. Since then, I purchased three more flips and each teaches me a new valuable lesson.

In 2019, I closed over 60 transactions and over $12,000,000 in volume. I am proud to say I now have a career total of over 300 homes sold and more than $65,000,000 in closed volume. I am ranked in the top 1% of all Realtors in the Philadelphia and Bucks County markets. I have been successfully flipping for two years now and this year I will start purchasing income properties to build a passive monthly income.

2014 seems like a lifetime ago. I have enjoyed the journey tremendously, because that is what life is all about. I encourage you to do the same! Remember, you are the *author* of your book in life, not the narrator. It is your action, or lack thereof, that puts you where you are today, and where you land tomorrow. No obstacle is too grand to overcome and turn into an opportunity and there is no better time than the present to realize this.

Rebecca L. Rynkiewicz

Rebecca Rynkiewicz is a Realtor that has been selling real estate since 2012. She works in Residential and Commercial Real Estate and is licensed in both PA and NJ. Rebecca is in the top 1% of agents in Philadelphia and surrounding counties, selling over $12,000,000 in properties in 2019, and a career total of over 300 homes sold. She started investing in real estate in 2018, flipping her first house, making a net profit of over $117,000, and continues to flip a house per quarter. In 2019 she began wholesaling, and successfully wholesaled her first deal making $70,000 in a single transaction. Growing up from humble beginnings, Rebecca is committed to inspiring others to live their dreams, setting massive goals, and taking massive action. When she is not working in the trenches of real estate, Rebecca's other passion is horses - and spends her time competing in the Adult Amateur Dressage Arena in Region 1 with her 12-year-old Dutch Warmblood gelding, Cowboy. Rebecca is also dedicated to raising money and donating to Last Chance Ranch, a 501(c)(3) nonprofit organization that saves animals from slaughter and neglect.

Storing Profits
By Corinn Altomare

*I must not fear. Fear is the mind-killer. Fear is the little-death that brings
total obliteration. I will face my fear. I will permit it to pass over me and
through me. And when it has gone past, I will turn the inner eye to see its
path. Where the fear has gone there will be nothing.*
Only I will remain.
-Frank Herbert

August 2019: As the general partner representing 15 passive investors
comprising our limited partners, I signed paperwork to acquire a 35,000
Net Rentable Square Feet (NRSF) self-storage facility in Lancaster
County, PA. Total project cost: $2,008,750.

Until this point I had worked as a classically trained musician, legal
secretary, IT project manager and property manager for my own real
estate investment portfolio. No clear career path to acquiring and
managing self-storage facilities in my work history. Yet, here I was. And
as it turns out, it was exactly those years of training and experience
across varied industries that lead me to this project.

Real Estate Investor

Seven years earlier, I had started real estate investing with a triplex, occupied with inherited tenants in two units. A few months later, I acquired another one with my then-boyfriend (now husband and business partner). We had a strong deal flow of smaller multi-family properties, so we continued acquiring through syndication. We started our company, Hearthfire Holdings, to manage the growing portfolio. Through hands-on management, we kept direct control over the investment performance while learning the operational foundations of successful real estate investing. We liked this investment strategy as a vehicle to build long-term wealth, not only for ourselves but also for our investors and their families. As we grew, we realized the challenge of managing operations across multiple smaller syndications, The Philadelphia MSA was booming in the multifamily sector, which led to properties being overpriced and more difficult to acquire. We would be able to build wealth faster by selling the smaller syndications, capturing the gains, and consolidating into a larger project. Moving into larger multi-family syndications would have been the logical choice, but we knew a market downturn was inevitable and wanted to introduce the recession resistance of self-storage (SS) into our portfolio. (See table below.) We laser-focused on hunting SS properties. We underwrote, bid and got outbid for approximately 18 months before going under contract. For us personally, our company and our investors, the project we acquired was perfectly timed and placed to diversify our overall holdings.

TOTAL ANNUAL RETURNS BY PROPERTY SECTOR					
Year	Office	Industrial	Retail	Apartments	Self Storage
5 yr Avg. Return '14-'18	11.8%	14.5%	4.7%	13.1%	14.1%
10 yr Avg. Return '09-'18	12.5%	13.7%	12.5%	15.9%	16.9%
15 yr Avg. Return '04-'18	9.8%	12.4%	9.4%	13.2%	16.5%
20 yr Avg. Return '99-'18	11.0%	13.8%	12.3%	13.6%	16.8%

Source Data: NAREIT

Recession Resistant	
Property Type	% In Returns (2007-2009)
Self Storage	-3.8%
Office	-8.2%
Retail	-12.3%
Industrial	-18.3%
Residential	-6.4%
Apartments	-6.7%
MHC	0.5%
Healthcare	4.9%
Mortgage	-19.5%
S&P 500	-22.0%

Source: NAREIT

Self-Storage Investor

Our primary reason for pivoting to SS at this time was its recession resistance. We had been at the height of an extended market upswing and were overdue for a downward correction. SS provides our overall investment portfolio with a stronger potential to navigate market cycles with minimal loss. (See graph on recession resistance measured by property type return in last down cycle, 2007-2009.)

We also like the lower maintenance and operation costs of SS compared to residential or commercial property management. SS has a break-even occupancy rate of 60-70%, and occupancy is considered stabilized at 85-90%. 90%+ occupancy means it's time to raise your rents. Compare this to the occupancy rates you would need on a single, multi-family or commercial property to protect and grow your original investment.

SS tenants are diverse – residential, business, short and long-term – minimizing investment risk. Residential tenants need SS whether upsizing, downsizing or moving. Business tenants pay a lower price per square foot for storage than they would for a commercial storefront or warehouse, so SS is an economical option for businesses in growth or decline.

On the topic of tenants – SS is a simpler model to operate here as well. There are fewer rent regulations, a straightforward process for handling late and non-payments, no fair housing laws, fewer tenant interactions and minimal turnover requirements. Compare the time and effort of a 2BD/1BA apartment turnover with that of a storage unit. Scaled up to 300 units, the difference is stark. In contrast to the TV popularity of "Storage Wars," auctions are increasingly run online. This maximizes advertising exposure, increases bid prices, minimizes risk and liability of crowds onsite, and removes the additional expense of an in-person auctioneer.

SS is not only real estate – it is a business, with opportunities to increase revenue through ancillary income streams. Merchandise sales (locks, packing materials), additional operating fees (administration, late, lock cut, auction), rentals (moving trucks, vans, labor) and tenant insurance are all great ways to maximize your investment performance.

Tenant insurance programs are a particularly strong option, balancing tenant relationship management with revenue management. It limits tenants' risk of loss while increasing revenue (facility receives a commission for participation in sales) and maintaining positive tenant relations. Should a loss occur, a tenant deals directly with the insurance company's claims department, not the facility.

Elaborating further on the opportunities of SS as a well-run business operation – use dynamic pricing models to maximize your facility revenue. A good management software will give you the capability to program these. Here are a few examples:

- Raise rates once occupancy reaches 90% of a specific unit mix (e.g., 10' x 10').
- Quote prices higher for walk-in customers (+15%) than online advertised specials.
- Higher prices (+5-15%) for "premium" units within a specific unit mix (e.g., on the end of an aisle, closer to gate entry)
- Multiple rate increase annually. (Your percentage and frequency here depend entirely upon your market, facility specifics and operator "buy-in." Some details from SS REITs: 8-12% every 9 months, with first increase six months after move-in. When I first heard this, my eyes popped! It is illuminating to find out how the major operators run their numbers.)

To see the immediate impact on the value of your business, here is a simple example.

ABC Storage raises its ancillary income of $1,000 per month, $12,000 per year.

Using a 6% cap rate, this additional $12,000 adds value of $200,000 to the business.

How?

Another attractive element to SS is the low barrier to entry. Much of the SS market is still held by individual operators. Out of the ~52,000 facilities in the market, only ~10,000 are owned and/or operated by larger companies. These companies show an appetite for large facilities and total store volume. This leaves opportunity in secondary or tertiary markets: investors can enter the asset class without ever having to compete with REITs/larger investors in the primary urban markets. And secondary/tertiary markets still present fantastic opportunities for cash flow, market cycle stability and building long-term wealth. Our acquisition met these criteria exactly: rural location owned and operated by an individual for 30+ years.

How to underwrite a SS offering? From a very high-level:

- Know your market. SS operates in one, three, and five-mile radii, give or take depending on population density. Rural markets have a broader market base: seven, ten, 20-mile radii. Know your competition, their occupancy and concessions and any potential new-build or expansion projects entering the market. Know your population trends, market demographics, and housing density. Know the supply number in your market. To calculate: NRSF (in your market) ÷ market population = Square Feet per Person. A balanced supply is generally calculated at 7.5 SQ FT/person. Higher = oversupply. Lower = undersupply.
- Business visibility/accessibility. Look for locations on high traffic volume roads. An easily accessible location improves the opportunity for ancillary revenue through moving truck rental (U-Haul, etc.)
- Know your market!

Operations

The months following settlement were demanding and filled with excitement. The facility had previously operated completely manually - with a handwritten ledger, receipts, lease signings, and no online presence. It was everything we could have hoped for in a value-add acquisition, and presented an opportunity uniquely met by our specific strengths: technology implementation and systematized operations. In our first months of operations we implemented:

- A comprehensive facility management platform, complete with dynamic unit pricing and revenue management, integrated tenant account management, auto bills and payment, SMS, email, and DocuSign templates for remote lease signing
- A full-service website, including online reservations and payments
- A new security system
- A new gate access system allowing for remote access and tracking tenant access
- Climate control unit conversion
- Conversion to LED lighting throughout the facility
- Retail sales
- A remodeled front office to deliver higher-quality experience to our customers and team members

It was not easy, but it was deeply rewarding to see such improvements realized in such a short amount of time. A few elements that deserve further elaboration:

Structure

Structurally, SS facilities are straightforward: steel and sheet metal structures on a concrete pad. You will have a few capital expenditures on a very predictable schedule. (Roof, grounds/paving, fencing, doors.) Compare this to the maintenance required of residential real estate: flooring, paint, plumbing and HVAC. Take this comparison another step further and consider the turnover process. For a residential turnover, the property owner will need to repair or replace any interior wear or damage. For commercial turnover, the property owner is often expected to provide build-to-suit conditions or Tenant Improvement (TI) funds. In the SS world, your turnover is much simpler: a quick sweep out and test that door and locks open and close smoothly.

The front building of our facility had been converted from a train station originally built in the 1800s. It makes an impressive historic statement, roots the facility within its immediate community and differentiates it from area competitors. The rear building is a standard concrete slab and metal build, surrounded by fence, gate, and lighting. We kept the remodel of the front building office simple and preserved the historic character, converted all lighting to LED, upgraded the existing gate system and scheduled a facelift for the grounds as weather conditions permitted.

This fundamental simplicity is getting a sexy upgrade though. Construction and technology advancements offer an entirely new user experience – smart lock systems, mobile access, self-serve kiosks, relocatable storage units and high-end fabricated construction materials (to name a few). While it didn't make sense for us to implement these offerings into our existing facility, you will find them in new-build and primary market facilities. It is only a matter of time before we see customer expectations drive the adoption of these amenities throughout the asset class.

Technology

Owner and customer expectations are driving technology adoption and implementation into SS operations. The next wave of SS owners expects automation efficiencies to drive down operational costs while maximizing occupancy and revenue. Today's customers expect to search "self-storage near me," narrow their options to the most convenient location and most affordable rate, and complete the move-in experience from their mobile device - all before showing up onsite with a moving truck.

To meet these expectations, we took our property management skill sets and adapted them for SS business operations. The primary high-level use cases are the same; advertise vacancies, attract tenants and collect rent. There are worlds of detail to unpack within each of these, of course!

With the deep integration of our software system and technology tools throughout our operations, we provide:

- A streamlined tenant experience (online reservation, payments, move-in, DocuSign)
- Remote capabilities, minimizing on-site staff requirements and cost overhead (self-guided access through the facility, remote control of gate system)
- Operator efficiency (central management of all facility components from the front office or remotely)
- Security control

People

There are three options for SS operations: on-site staff, technology-driven with no staff on-site and a hybrid approach – with technology as the backbone (such as a self-serve kiosk, remote lock/unlock capabilities, etc.), offsite call center and onsite staff limited to necessary grounds, security and maintenance checks. If the SS facility requires staff on-site, hiring the right talent is crucial to your investment performance. Operators must possess a unique mix of talents spanning sales, revenue management, marketing, technology, great attitude (even in the face of belligerent delinquent tenants) and the ability to perform janitorial tasks. In new-build SS facilities, the staff must have all the traits above, plus a solid understanding of technology and a curiosity to learn the forever changing technological enhancements.

Summary

SS has attracted increasing interest over recent years, with large institutional investors and REITs entering the space. A high volume of new construction has driven up vacancy rates and glutted markets. However, according to Moody's Analytics REIS tracking of new units projected to come online in 2020, the vacancy rate is projected to flatten out and then fall back closer to 2021.

Self-storage construction spending by year

Given these indicators and projections, there is still an opportunity for individual investors to find projects that would not attract larger investment entities: <30,000 Net Rentable Square Feet (NRSF), in secondary or tertiary markets. While cash flow and long-term wealth-building are still achievable with these criteria, the numbers simply are not big enough to be attractive to the larger players. By implementing new technologies and ancillary income streams and maximizing business operational efficiencies, the individual investor still has a great opportunity to achieve wealth through self-storage.

If you're working too hard for too little profit in overheated markets, step back and consider pivot points. I never expected my journey into self-storage, regret none of it, and the twists and turns have made for a grand adventure along the way.

Corinn Altomare

Corinn Altomare is a classically trained musician turned real estate investor. During her professional career as an opera singer, she performed a diverse range of repertoire spanning the Baroque period to contemporary, from pop-up locations in city centers to reverent chapels nestled within European countrysides. After 13 years as a vagabond musician Corinn was ready for a new challenge. She found this - ultimately - in real estate. Corinn comes from entrepreneurial parents - her mother founded and ran a Montessori preschool, her father a family and financial planning law practice. Her youngest childhood memories are of accompanying them on daily operations. This early exposure served Corinn well as she pivoted to the realm of IT project management for five years. This time was marked by continual growth, training and development in a world completely different from her previous artistic and entrepreneurial ones.

Corinn's next career shift was into real estate investing. As an individual investor, she acquired a triplex in the Francisville neighborhood of Philadelphia. This purchase was followed closely by multiple others within a few very busy years, acquired through syndication with - at first - close friends and family. She jumped into her new roles of owner and property manager across a quickly growing portfolio. She started her company, Hearthfire Holdings, with her now-husband and business partner. While only dating at the time, after navigating a few investment property purchases, landlord and hands-on repairs and maintenance together, they knew a formal partnership - in life and business - was in order.

Hearthfire Holdings made a strategic pivot into self-storage after seven years in residential real estate. This decision was made largely upon the assessment of an overheated, overextended market high and the recognition of an inevitable downward correction. This move turned out to be made just in time, given the impact of COVID-19 on our global economy in 1Q2020. Pre-planning for this shift started in 2017, and Hearthfire Holdings sold off smaller syndications 4Q2018-1Q2019, delivering investor returns of 23-24% IRR. Funds from these sales were consolidated into a successful acquisition of a 35,000 net rentable square feet self-storage facility in Lancaster County, PA, in 3Q2019. Hearthfire Holdings maintains a portfolio of commercial and residential multifamily properties in the Philadelphia MSA, which with their self-storage facility represents a total portfolio valuing $9M.

Acting on Conviction
By Kathy Fettke

Most of the important things in the world have been accomplished by people who kept on trying when there seemed to be no hope at all.
-Dale Carnegie

I was cooking dinner one evening back in 2013 when my husband walked into the kitchen. I looked up to say hello and was shocked to see he had tears in his eyes. I gasped. "What's wrong?!"

He paused, and then whispered, "The doctor told me I have 6 months to live."

Rich had just returned from the doctor to check on a freckle. The tests confirmed it was melanoma, a deadly skin cancer that appeared to have spread to his liver.

We were in total shock.

Rich had just completed a national book tour for his new book, *Extreme Success*. He had a full business coaching practice with a waitlist. We had two healthy, young daughters, and owned a new 4000 square foot home. We were living the dream...and suddenly, that dream turned into a real-life nightmare.

I refused to believe the doctor. Instead, I committed to myself to take over the finances so Rich could relax and get better. I had no idea how to do any of it.

The next months were tough. I didn't know how to make money anymore because I had been a stay-at-home mom for years. My prior career had been in broadcast news, and I kept a weekend radio show in San Francisco for fun, but without pay.

I applied for a job at a non-profit. I cried during the interview when I realized I'd have to leave my young kids all day. I guess they thought it was cute, so they hired me anyway. But, soon, one day when I walked into the office five minutes late, after a challenging morning of trying to get the girls off to school on time. My manager looked at her watch and then looked at me with a frown.

I thought angrily, "You don't own me!" And then I realized, "Oh, maybe you do - at least between the hours of 9 and 5." I quit.

I had just found out from a friend I could make $600 per month providing room and board to exchange students, per bed! We had a huge playroom upstairs I quickly turned into a boarding room with two bunk beds. We also turned an office in the house into a separate unit and rented that out, along with another "granny" unit.

Soon I was making more money renting out space in our home than that slave-job provided, however, it came at a cost. I had to prepare dinners for eight instead of four people, and often was waiting in line for the bathroom, but it was worth it.

That extra rental income paid our mortgage, allowing us to keep our house. And luckily, we did because, during that time, home values started to soar in California.

The rental income also allowed me to stay at home and still be a mom. Since I had some free time during the day while the kids were at school, I tried to find more ways to make money during those hours.

I still had that weekend radio show, so I thought I would try to make money from it. I listened to other radio shows on the same station to find out who was advertising. It seemed that nearly every ad at the time was for mortgages.

I grabbed the phone book (remember those?) and found a list of local mortgage brokers. I called each one asking if they would like to sponsor my show. Each one politely declined.

I knew I was doing something wrong because obviously, they were willing to sponsor other shows. I decided the next call I would make would result in a "YES!" That would require that I make an offer that could not be refused. The next name on the list was Cobblestone Mortgage in Danville. I dialed the number and Gary Massari answered.

"Gary? This is Kathy Fettke from KNEW in San Francisco. I have a radio show on Saturdays, and I'd like you to be my co-host."

Gary said, "Sounds great. When can we meet?"

I met with him the next day, showed him what it would cost to give him incredible exposure, and he wrote the check that day. I had my first sponsor.

I came home and told my husband I now had a mortgage show. He burst out laughing and said, "Well, you just lost your audience.

But then he gave it a bit more thought and said, "Why don't you cover human interest stories instead of talking rates like everyone else is doing? Find out what his clients are doing with the mortgages."

Did I mention my husband is a brilliant marketer? And, did I mention he is perfectly healthy today? The doctor was wrong, thankfully! But during the months of uncertainty, I discovered something within myself I might never have found had it not been for this crisis.

The most difficult times in life are often the moments that force us to get off our butts and create miracles. Otherwise, as creatures of habit, we might as well just keep doing the same old thing forever, even if that same old thing is not exactly what we want.

I interviewed Gary's mortgage clients and a whole new world opened for me. I learned how one guy got a loan for an old house, borrowed enough to also fix it up, and then sold it for a big profit. I interviewed another guy who bought a four-plex with one loan, rented the other 3 units and lived for free in the fourth unit because the other rents covered all his expenses. I found out a single woman was able to acquire an unlimited number of loans to buy properties she could rent out for far more than the mortgage, taxes and insurance cost. She retired early because of the extra cash flow, while her tenants were paying her mortgages off for her.

"Why didn't anyone tell me about this before?" I wondered. And, apparently, my audience was thinking the same thing.

Soon Gary's phones were ringing off the hook. He had so many people wanting to get mortgages he could not keep up. He soon asked me if I would get my real estate license so I could take these new clients. I agreed and had my real estate license the next month.

I was soon one of the busiest mortgage brokers in the San Francisco Bay Area. My first client wanted to do a million-dollar refinance. He came to our meeting, pulled out a folder, opened it up and spread his entire financial history in front of me. He said, "What do you recommend I do so that I can retire in a few years?"

I stared at him blankly and then politely excused myself. I had no idea what he should do! I grabbed my boss and brought him back into the room to help. It was then that I realized even highly successful people did not really know what to do with their money.

That is when I made it my mission to bring the secrets of the wealthy to the rest of us. I renamed the radio show the "RealWealth Show" and interviewed "real" people who had created enormous wealth. I was shocked at how much they would share.

The RealWealth Show took off. This was before podcasts, so getting secrets from the wealthy was very difficult at the time. As I became more well-known in the San Francisco Bay Area, I started getting invited to speak at Real Estate Investment Clubs. Soon I realized those clubs made their money by taking 50% of the profits from the sale of the speaker's expensive boot camps. Unfortunately, many of those boot camps were expensive, often outdated, and very cheesy.

Rich and I created our own events with no high pressured, back-of-the-room sales. We named the group the "RealWealth Network." We wanted a safe place for people to learn real information about how to build wealth from a network of experienced experts, without having to buy anything.

My mortgage business kept booming as a result, but I also was very confused by it. Why were the banks letting me give loans to nearly anyone, without any proof of their ability to pay them back? I could literally give someone an application, let them fill it out, and not have to verify any of it. It just didn't make sense.

I interviewed Robert Kiyosaki, the author of *Rich Dad Poor Dad* on my show. During our interview, I asked him what he thought about the crazy loans banks were allowing. He said it was a disaster and that people won't be able to pay them back. He also said that easy money was driving real estate values up past affordable levels and that the housing bubble would pop as soon as people realized they could not pay the loans back. It made so much sense, yet so many people could not see it.

I asked Robert what he was doing with his money. He said he sold all his properties in high priced bubble markets like California and was exchanging them for high cash flow properties in Texas, tax-deferred (through a 1031 exchange).

I asked, "Why Texas?" He explained that it had the largest job and population growth in the country, but properties were still affordable.

This made sense, so I booked a trip to Dallas. First, I met with a real estate agent I found online. She took me to the most expensive neighborhoods and said, "Californians like this area."

Homes were $400,000 there, but I knew the median home price in Dallas was around $140,000. That is when I learned the importance of only working with agents who understood investing.

I found a wonderful agent/property manager who knew the importance of buying low-cost properties that cash flow (meaning the rents exceed all monthly expenses). She took me to an area where brand new homes were around $145,000 in A-class neighborhoods with great schools that rented for over $1500 per month.

I also learned from her that if you want appreciation on top of cash flow, buy property in the "path of progress." Rockwall, TX was one of those places. It was an adorable town but had a long commute to jobs because you had to drive around a lake to get there. She let me know that a new freeway was planned that would cut the commute time in half.

Rich and I refinanced the house in California we managed to keep and ended up using the cash as down payments on five new homes in Rockwall. When I talked about it on the RealWealth Show, people called in and mocked us.

"Texas? Nothing happens in Texas!"

"The property taxes will kill your cash flow."

"Why would you leave a dynamic California market for a boring Texas market?"

"There's nothing but land in Texas. Values will never increase."

These critics simply could not see what had become so clear to us. We were buying quality homes in desirable neighborhoods near massive job growth and new infrastructure. And those homes would be managed by an experienced property manager. I could not see a downside.

Some of my show listeners could see it. One woman heard me talk about my Texas properties on the RealWealth Show and called in to find out more. She told me she wanted to retire, but bought three rental properties in Stockton, CA that were not getting her there. While they were worth about $400,000 each, they only rented for $1200 each. Plus, they constantly needed repairs because they were old and had high turnover rates because they were in a bad part of town.

I helped her sell them to acquire nine new properties in Rockwall, Texas. She quadrupled her cash flow in that one exchange and discovered she was finally able to retire on the cash flow. Plus, she no longer had to deal with bad tenants or constant repairs because she traded old homes in bad areas for quality homes in better neighborhoods. Any future repairs would be handled by a property manager, not her. She thanked me profusely for the freedom she could now enjoy.

When I interviewed her on the show, some people thought I had really put her in danger. "A retiree owning property out of state? That's dangerous!"

About 18 months later, Lehman Brothers collapsed, and property values plummeted nationwide. The Stockton properties she sold for $400,000 each were soon worth about $75,000. Her Texas properties never lost their value, and the rents continued to rise, even during the greatest housing collapse since the Great Depression. In fact, she never even felt the Great Recession. Today, her properties are worth three to four times what she paid.

Unfortunately, I didn't always follow my own advice. I got too confident and searched out another market to diversify. I saw an article that listed Boise, Idaho as one of the hottest up and coming real estate markets in the country. I jumped on a plane headed to Boise and came back with three new rental properties.

I bought them more with the hope of appreciation in value than for cash flow, which turned out to be highly speculative. I also broke my basic investing rules. Boise was a small city with only a handful of major employers, and yet it was not particularly affordable at the time. Plus, I self-managed the properties when I didn't fully understand the local market.

When the real estate market collapsed in 2008, so did rents and property values in Boise. That was a tough lesson. We were feeding those properties for years to keep them alive, (otherwise known as negative cash flow). We could not sell them because there was no market at the time. We ended up having to do short sales, which destroyed our credit.

By this time, RealWealth Network had grown into thousands of members worldwide and the RealWealth Show was among the top 10 real estate podcasts on iTunes, but I felt like a total failure. I only had myself to blame, because I did not even follow my own advice. Our RealWealth members who bought in Dallas fared very well throughout the recession, while I was just trying to keep my head above water with a few properties I never should have bought.

Remember, it's the hard times that define us.

As foreclosures mounted nationwide, I knew it was time to buy, even if I could not take advantage of the opportunities myself.

Thankfully, I was able to help others. Right around Christmas in 2009, I got a call from a woman who ran an investor group in Australia. She wanted to know if I could help her clients find property in the U.S. I told her I absolutely could. A few weeks later, I was on a stage in Sydney, speaking to a thousand Australian investors eager to come to America.

The Australian dollar had nearly doubled during the recession, while U.S. property values had tanked. It was the opportunity of a lifetime for Australians to buy American real estate at a discount.

I quickly found real estate agents and wholesalers across the country who specialized in finding foreclosures. I also found property managers who could renovate the properties, place qualified tenants and offer ongoing management. The "turn-key rental model" was born.

Australians could not believe they could buy renovated properties for under $50,000. For the next few years, we hosted bus tours packed with investors who wanted to buy properties in Kansas City, Indianapolis, Cleveland, Pittsburgh, Atlanta, Dallas and Tampa. These investors were willing to buy stinky, boarded up homes in distressed neighborhoods, fix them up and street by street, improve some of the hardest-hit neighborhoods in America.

In 2012, I opened the mail to find a letter from Goldman Sachs. At first, I thought it was a joke, so I tossed it. But my daughter, who was interning for me at the time, pulled it out of the garbage and saw it was signed by CEO Lloyd Blankfein. It turned out Goldman Sachs was honoring me as one of their 100 Most Intriguing Entrepreneurs at the upcoming Builders and Innovators Summit. I accepted.

When I pulled up at the event, I was handed a glass of champagne as I stepped out of the car and greeted by several men in suits. Stunned, I asked how I was chosen for this honor. One man replied, "For your work in helping clean up the foreclosure crisis." The wind blew, and the name tag spun around so I could read it. It was Lloyd Blankfein!

I was ushered to the welcome party and introduced to the other honorees, who ranged from the founders of Uber to Soul Cycle, Kind, and even Elon Musk, the owner of Tesla! It was surreal. After three days of conferencing with these great innovators, I left realizing the importance of what had seemed so basic before: providing affordable housing to American families.

The Wall Street Journal interviewed me at that event and shared what we were doing. It may have been that article that led to the next exciting phone call I received.

Fox News called, asking if I would debate Robert Schiller on live T.V. Yes, the same Robert Schiller of the Case Shiller Index and Nobel Prize winner for economics. He was of the belief it was a dangerous time to buy real estate. I accepted the challenge.

During that interview, Mr. Schiller was concerned that prices might continue to fall as they had for the past few years. I argued that interest rates were at all-time lows, along with home prices, and owning a home in most markets was about a third cheaper than renting. I exclaimed that it was the greatest opportunity to build wealth ever! In the end, he agreed with me.

How Did I Know This?

Common sense. You do not need a Yale degree to know that if you can buy a property for less than its replacement cost, and charge rent that is much higher than your expenses, in a market growing and redefining itself, you get cash flow today and the potential for appreciation in the future. Those $50,000 properties grew two to three times in value in just a few years.

But as more investors jumped in, prices eventually bounced back to 2006 levels. It became more and more difficult to find good deals, and many people overpaid for properties. At RealWealth, we knew a correction was coming, and prepared for it. In fact, in my 2020 Housing Forecast, I predicted a Black Swan event would change everything. I did not expect that just a few months later, over 20 million people would lose their jobs in a matter of weeks due to Coronavirus fears.

We do not know how long the recession will last, but we are certain that the need for affordable housing has become stronger than ever. That means the opportunity to build wealth in real estate is as strong as ever.

At RealWealth, we continue to focus on the same fundamentals we have recommended since the beginning. We help people acquire rental properties in areas with these important elements in place:

- Housing affordability (home prices and rents no more than 3 times incomes)
- Steady job growth with a strong diversification of employment
- Population growth
- City redevelopment plans
- At least 1 million people in the metro area

• Landlord-friendly rent laws

Starting in March of 2020 when the virus hit the news, our strategy was tested. We immediately gathered all 15 property managers in our network on Zoom to share tips and strategies on how they can take care of both tenants and landlords during the coming months.

We've been shocked to learn that despite the massive job losses, nearly all the property managers in our network have collected over 95% of rents and received an *increase* of qualified applications! How could this be?

It seems that once again, housing has moved to the top of the list of priorities. "Stay at home orders" make the need for a comfortable home even more important these days. Even during past recessions, rents did not dip much. Having a home takes priority over all other expenses.

The way the government is responding to this crisis could also benefit real estate in the long run. One of the ways the Federal Reserve boosts an economy is through stimulus. There has never been a time in the past when the Federal Reserve stimulated the economy quite to this level.

When money is printed, paper loses value while real estate and other hard assets increase in value. That is why property and stock values increased so much after the Great Recession when the Fed ushered in years of quantitative easing combined with low-interest rates. Gold is another asset class that increases in value during recessions, and while that can be a haven for investors, it does not cash flow like real estate does.

If you have more time than money, you may want to learn how to wholesale. This means you find property at a discount and find a buyer who wants to buy property at a discount. You charge a fee for the deal, even if you have none of your own money in it.

You could also get your real estate license and learn about short sales or finding foreclosed properties at auctions. If you become an expert at finding good deals, you will likely also find investors with the money to invest in those deals.

If you have more money than time, consider buy and hold rental properties. You can get up to ten loans through Fannie Mae or Freddie Mac at record low rates today, which will further increase your cash flow. As more people tap into their savings, they may be unable to own a home in the coming years, and instead will be forced to rent.

If you are buying out of state, like I do, make sure you hire a licensed inspector to verify the condition of the property before closing. It is worth the money to pay for a third-party appraisal as well to verify the value.

If you thought you missed the opportunity to invest in real estate because prices got so high in 2019, now is your chance. This would be a very good time to understand how to acquire property in a down market.

Since we get about 1000 new members at RealWealth every month who want to learn how to invest in real estate, I am guessing I am not alone in this thinking.

Kathy Fettke

Kathy Fettke is Co-CEO of RealWealth and best-selling author of *Retire Rich with Rentals*. She is an active real estate investor, licensed real estate agent, and former mortgage broker, specializing in helping people build multi-million-dollar real estate portfolios that generate passive monthly cash flow for life.

With a passion for researching real estate market cycles, Kathy is a frequent guest expert on CNN, CNBC, Fox, Bloomberg, NPR, CBS MarketWatch and the Wall Street Journal. She was also named among the "Top 100 Most Intriguing Entrepreneurs" by Goldman Sachs two years in a row.

Kathy hosts two podcasts, The Real Wealth Show and Real Estate News for Investors — both top ten podcasts on iTunes with listeners in 133 countries. Her company, RealWealth, offers free resources and cutting-edge education for beginning and experienced real estate investors. Kathy is passionate about teaching others how to create "real wealth," which she defines as having both the time and the money to live life on your terms.

Network Your Way to Millions
By April Crossley

No one is going to stand up at your funeral and say: "She had a really expensive couch and great shoes." Don't make life about stuff.
–Bernadette Leite

Borrowing and lending private money reminds me of dating. At first, the borrower and lender are not sure how to find each other. They are both looking but do not want to seem desperate and are unsure of where to start. Maybe friends will connect you? Maybe you should join some type of website? Maybe you should actively seek each other out? Then, once you find each other, you slowly feel each other out to see if you connect. I do not care how much money you have, if I do not like you, I am not dating... ummm... I mean borrowing... money from you. If you do connect and trust is built, you tell each other what you need. Then you tiptoe into a relationship together and if it goes well, you become obsessed with each other and how awesome things are, and you want to be the ONLY ONE this person works with!

Yeah... pretty much just like dating.

For 12 years I have flipped houses and purchased all my rental portfolio with other people's money. It was how I started, and I did not know any other way. I did not understand how to work with a bank. People would tell me they use their own money to buy houses and my response was always, "Ewwww, that is so gross. Why would you do that??!!!"

It is hard to buy houses with your own money when you do not have any. And, by none, I mean zero. I was a teenage mom on food stamps, turned healthcare worker, turned real estate investor with college debt, rent to pay and was just discovering the world of real estate. All I knew was how to find deals, so that is all I did. When I finally found a deal, I had no idea how I would buy it. I took it to someone that knew how to buy. They offered to do a joint venture. We would both buy the deal and split the profit. They would bring the money and we would bring the sweat equity (that is a nice way of saying I got sweaty to save a buck by doing things we did not need to pay a contractor to do). The deal went great! And, at the end, everyone got paid. Including someone I had never met.

It turns out, that my partner on the deal did not bring his own money to the deal; *he brought someone else's money to the deal!* That someone was a guy that just loaned money out to real estate flippers to make a good return. He did not have to look for deals, or put in sweat equity, or deal with contractors or sellers. All he did was write checks and make a great return on his money. At the end of our joint venture deal, this guy told us if we were going to do more deals in the future, to come to him for money. So, we did! In the dating world, we would call him: A fast mover. In his defense, he already got to see how we performed on a successful project, so he knew what he was getting himself into. As I continued to borrow money from my first lender, I realized that his funds limited me to three houses a year. Fortunately, I only needed to flip three houses a year to leave my healthcare job, and for years, I did just that.

When I started borrowing money, I was not a big thinker. To this day, I do not consider myself a big thinker. I really must push myself to get into rooms with people who think bigger and are more creative than I. I did this by joining masterminds. Once I went to Meetup groups, surrounding myself with big thinkers and reading more books, I realized the more money I had, the more deals I could do! It also dawned on me that some people had no idea how to find deals, but I did! So, I became an off-market deal-finding master. I decided if I can find deals this way, I can find money this way too!

When I set out to find more money, I was reading this amazing book called *Getting the Money* by Susan Lassiter-Lyons. She had raised millions in private funds, and I wanted to do the same. I did everything she told me. It is amazing how that works when you follow someone's advice that has done something before you instead of re-inventing the wheel. Listen to people who are where you want to be and act on what they tell you! I also hired a coach to help me think a little bigger and find more money. To this day, the following are still my top five ways I have used and continue to use, to network my way to millions in private money.

1. Joint Venture: Newbies often ask me why any private lender would trust them if they have never done a deal before? Truth is, they probably will not. If they do, they will probably charge you a ridiculously high-interest rate to hedge their risk. The fastest way to get in with one is to do a joint venture on a deal with a more experienced investor. As a private lender myself, I often will offer to joint venture with newbies on deals. Or I ask them to joint venture with someone with more experience. Even as an experienced flipper, private lender and rental property owner – as I grow up in the real estate world and buy bigger things like mobile home parks, storage facilities, etc. I do not expect someone to just give me a loan and trust I know what I am doing with these types of investments. I must prove myself. I must team up with someone who has experience in these areas to build knowledge and trust. A joint venture is a great way to show someone how valuable you can be to a deal. So, where do you find great joint venture partners? It is just like dating! You go somewhere where people flipping houses hang out! No, not the bar! Yes, real estate can be stressful, but there are better places! Local Real Estate Investment Groups in your area are a great start! You can search for them on social media or look on www.meetup.com Just like dating, you go, mingle, chat and see who you connect with that seems trustworthy. Go with your gut; it never lies!

2. Networking at Real Estate Investment Meetup Groups/Seminars: I organize a meetup group in my area with 1,400 members. Every month we hold a meeting and at least three to five of my private lenders are in the room. They do not stand up and wave their hands and say, "Hey! I have private money!" Well... some do... but most do not. They do not want to get bombarded by people who supposedly have deals that are not really deals. Private lending is also very relationship and trust-based, so they want to get to know you first. Often, they will just introduce themselves to you as an investor and ask you about yourself. Be authentic! Be honest! Talk about what you do even if you are a newbie. At a recent meeting, one of my private lenders said:

My Lender: "April, do you know Stacey? She is over there with the brown hair."

Me: "Yeah, really nice girl."

My lender: "We really seem to click; I think I'm going to tell her I am a private lender!"

ME: "Yes! You should! You two would work well together!"

See what I mean? Just like dating. As much as you are looking for private lenders, they are also looking for you!

3. Direct Mail: Everyone talks about direct mail for finding sellers, but never for finding private lenders. I send letters to people I find through public records and list broker sites, to absentee owners and people that have previously done private loans in my area. I seek them out based on their interests and hobbies. Just like dating, I want this person to have something in common with me. WHY? Because it makes building rapport and networking with them SO much easier! For example, my husband and I ride motorcycles. I send direct mail to people who invest in real estate and ride motorcycles. In my direct mail, I do not ask them for money. I just simply state I noticed they were in real estate and would love to connect and invite them for coffee. Inevitably, at the coffee meeting we talk about why we love real estate and other things we do for fun. I will always ask, "Other than real estate, what do you do for fun?" They will say, "Well, I ride motorcycles." Which I follow up with, "NO WAY! My husband and I ride motorcycles too!!" This leads to a whole conversation and relationship building revolving around similar interests. It makes networking easy. I already knew they rode motorcycles because I targeted them due to that fact, but they do not know that! Just instant rapport. Coffee meetings with other investors have been great for me to find private money. I have met a lot of investors this way that own their own rentals and flip houses and have lots of money. They had no idea what a private lender was, or that they could make money simply by lending on a deal without having to do anything else. I have turned flippers and landlords into private lenders. Do not assume just because someone has experience in real estate they know what private lending is. Lots of people only know one way to buy, and that is with their own money. Once educated on private lending, a lot of these investors realize they do not want the headaches of chasing deals and dealing with tenants and end up loving private lending.

4. On-Site Rehab Project Meetings: These days, everyone thinks they want to be a house flipper. They do not understand it is a full-time job of finding deals, working with contractors… the list goes on. Many people think because they have some extra money lying around that they should flip houses to grow that money as fast as possible. I like to show them the reality of house flipping. I open my flip projects to them. I invite people to my rehab projects to learn about how I found the deal, rehabbed the house and funded the deal. I post on social media about it and in my meetup group and anyone/everyone is welcome. During the meeting, I focus on the hurdles with the project and how easy it was for my private lender to make a great return without having to do anything but write a check. Inevitably, at the end of every meeting, someone comes up to me and says: "Wow, I never heard of private lending! That seems SO much easier than finding houses and flipping them. I have money, can you tell me more about that?" This, of course, instantly leads scheduling a coffee date with them.

5. Social Media Posts: This is for the introverts out there that hate networking. Talking about what you do on social media is one of the easiest ways to get people to inquire. Note I did NOT say asking for money on social media. Do not ask for money. We educate. Educate people about real estate investing and what we do during our day-to-day. For instance, I may post a picture of a house and say, "People always think I must be rich because I have all this money to buy real estate. The fact is, I could never make it in this business without my private lenders. Kudos to them for putting their old 401k, IRAs, and savings account money to work for them to make them more money. Real Estate investors and Private Lenders make the best team!" When you post something like this and talk about your day to day people start asking: Why? How? And your next step after they inquire is to invite them to coffee… just like you would do if you were dating!

As someone who has utilized private money for all her deals over the past 12 years, and now as a private lender myself, I truly have an appreciation for how relationship-based this business is. Private lenders are looking for you as much as you are looking for them. They want to work with people they connect with, just like you do! Doing business is great, but doing business with people you enjoy being around is even better! Do not put too much pressure on yourself when looking for private money lenders. Just get out there and be your authentic self! They will be doing the same! Together you will help each other grow wealth with real estate!

April Crossley

April Crossley is a no-nonsense educator and investor who helps people grow wealth with real estate. She began investing in 2004 when she started flipping houses as a side gig. Her first deal was completed on a joint venture with other people's money. Since 2004 April has only purchased deals off market and has never used any of her own money to buy her flip projects or rental properties. She has raised millions in private funds and has trusted relationships with dozens of private lenders she works with regularly. She flips and wholesales between 20- 30 houses a year, owns a portfolio of small multifamily rental properties in Berks County, PA and she is also a private lender. April retired at 35 from a 13-year long career in healthcare by investing in real estate. She lives in Berks County, PA and lives part time during the winter in Arizona. Since the start of her career, she has helped a multitude of people retire from their careers early by teaching them how to flip houses or become private lenders via her consulting company Lazy Girl REI. April also organizes a real estate investment group in Berks County, PA with 1,400 members and her YouTube Channel with over 10,000 subscribers she utilizes to help spread her message about growing wealth with real estate, so more people can have financial freedom. She is passionate about helping other people grow wealth with real estate by helping them find the path best for them: flipping vs. owning rental property vs. private lending. April speaks frequently on podcast interviews and at conferences about her journey from being a teenage mom on welfare to starting in healthcare, and then transitioning into a life of financial freedom through real estate.

Going Alone
By Maria Friström

*Never follow anyone else's path, unless you're in the woods and you're lost
and you see a path. Then by all means follow that path.*
-Ellen DeGeneres

The Tough Mudder

Have you heard of the Tough Mudder race? It is a 14-mile run over
a mountain with 20 army grade obstacles you haul yourself over and
under like a freakin' Marvel superhero. I am a former 400m runner
and running even that made me hurl. I did not think I was physically
capable of running over five miles. Let alone a half marathon over a
father-mucking mountain. But I did. While pregnant.

Now, what the hell does this have to do with real estate investing, and
you? Well, do you ever feel overwhelmed? Like your project is crap—
and that you are crap? And certain that you will never be able to get
finished, or started even, because it feels like…well…climbing a damn
mountain as a walrus? I know you can, and in this chapter, I will tell you
a couple of ways how.

A Lactation Epiphany

In the summer of 2016, I suddenly found myself locked in the company massage room, hooked onto a machine that sucked the youth and glory out of my knockers, a.k.a. a breast pump. If you have never used or seen a breast pump on full speed and max suction power, you have missed out. And are blessed. Because it is as funny as it is degrading and quite frankly a scary sight. I wanted to add a note on the door saying: "Do you want nightmares for the rest of your life, and never want to have sex again? Please enter." Sorry cows, for all the wrong we have done to your nipples. I will never drink milk again.

I had given birth to Lucas, our first-born, and returned to work after the longest maternity leave in the 25-year-history of the Silicon Valley-based company—5 months. I loved my job, but this moment clarified it: I cannot be working like this and pay a big portion of my salary to somebody else to raise my kids. Enter real estate investing.

Donkeywork

The first portion of the Tough Mudder in Lake Tahoe is straight up the ski slope. The race literally starts mid-slope. It is not the kiddy slope, but the "skull and crossbones" slope. A lot of ACLs have lost their lives on that slope, may they rest in peace in ligament heaven. When the starting pistol went off, we began climbing. And I mean climbing because it was so steep, I had to use my arms and hands to pull myself up the slope. But next to me, I saw some jogging, and the strongest and fittest racers were miraculously running up that bad boy. Like, what in the actual hell?

In my first year of real estate investing, I bought 100 units, made a gazillion dollars and did it all while standing on my head. Not. Do you ever get the feeling when reading success stories it all sounds too good to be true? That it is so inspirational, it becomes demotivating? Well, I want to keep it real with you. Shifting into real estate investing was hard and still is. Much like climbing a mountain with 20 army grade obstacles while pregnant (see what I did there). A lot of my offers get declined, deals fall through, appraisals come in lower than I hoped, I drill holes in the wrong place (I mean WTAF), my DIY projects come out like the ugly cousin to the Pinterest inspiration pic and I compare myself to other investors who all seem to jog up that mountain like there is nothing to it while I am down on my hands and knees crawling.

Do Your Thang

Since my lactation epiphany of getting into real estate investing, we moved to Finland, and had another baby. They are 15 months apart. During that time I have not bought 100 apartments while standing on my head, but I have built a rental portfolio worth over a million dollars hauling two babies (at first in my belly, then hanging on to my nips), using the Buy, Rehab, Rent, Refinance, and Repeat (BRRRR) method. *Thanks for coining that Brandon Turner, you are an actual word-wizard (his beard beats Gandalf's all day).* It has been awesome, and I have also screamed a lot into pillows, and aged about 320 years.

Before I tell you how I did this—and how you can too—I must tell you this story. I was born in Finland but raised in Sweden. English is my third language. In 2011 I worked at one of the world's leading communication agencies in Silicon Valley...I realize this sounds so dreamy...and kind of pompous. But know this: I started my communication career with selling cigarettes. Literally. I was a cig-girl at clubs. So do not compare my chapter 20 to your chapter one. I am like 100 years old and have had a long monkey-gym career. Now, where was I? Oh yeah...I was self-conscious about my Swenglish. I compensated it with working like crazy and being super professional, a.k.a. boring. I didn't bring the real me to the table.

Until this one day. A client phone call. I decided to break out of my robot shell and be myself. This is how it played out. We were in the conference room, the entire team there with me: my project manager, our content developer, designer and art director. I dial the number and as we wait for the client to pick up, I declare to the team: "From now on I will say the word "balls" on every client call." The client picks up and I say: "blah, blah, blah, so what are your thoughts on how far you want to push this presentation? Do you want to keep it pretty close to what it is, or do you want to go BALLS to the wall?" *mic drop*

Now, I am not saying that everybody should go around saying "balls" on client calls. For me, being me, just means making people laugh, being serious about work, but not taking things too seriously, and to push boundaries. Here is how finding the courage to do me has played out in my real estate investing.

How Can I?

When we moved to Finland, I was already gung-ho about real estate. Luckily, I had a great job and a lot of experience. Except that I did not. I had left my job in California and I knew nothing about the Finnish real estate market. My network consisted of an eight-month-old parkour baby and an alien in my belly. My husband traveled 150 days a year and my family lived far away.

One thing that is challenging in Finland is home sale prices are not available to the public. This makes it difficult to know the value of a home, since no comparable pricing "comp" is available. Knowing if a deal is good or a pig in a sack takes a lot of market knowledge, or an awesome network. Great, I had none.

So, I gave up and started a career in collecting belly button lint instead. The end. Nah, instead of thinking "I can't" I, Miss Runs-Until-She-Hurls, set my brain on problem-solving mode by asking "how can I?" and came up with this way to get around it.

I chose my areas of focus based on my goals and strategy I had developed according to the teachings in the book, "The Millionaire Real Estate Investor" by Gary Keller, Dave Jenks and Jay Papasan and started analyzing deals. Several a day. I wrote them all down in an excel. All the info a comp would include. In three months, I had a pretty good sense of what "a good deal" looked like. I basically created my own comps based on the asking price.

Hawt Hawt Hawt

When I started investing in Finland, the market here in Helsinki was hot like shirtless Brad Pitt.

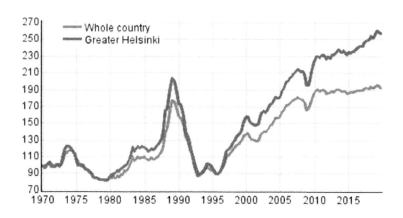

Official Statistics of Finland (OSF): Prices of dwellings in housing companies [e-publication]. ISSN=2323-8801. February 2020, Appendix figure 5. Real Price Index of old dwellings in blocks of flats, index 1970=100. Helsinki: Statistics Finland [referred: 13.4.2020]. Access method: http://www.stat.fi/til/ashi/2020/02/ashi_2020_02_2020-03-31_kuv_005_en.html

The market was flooded by investor-competition. A lot of private and institutional investors offered brand new apartments to tenants. I could not compete with the perks offered by the institutional investors (like a car) thanks to their economies of scale. I could not compete with the private investors with tons of experience and a massive network...Yet! But I could do one thing others couldn't. I could do me. Bring out the ballsy.

After three months of analyzing deals and looking at the rental supply, I noticed that they all looked the same. The new-builds all had white walls, white kitchens, and the same cookie-cutter materials. The others were run down, and they all looked like they were designed by...well... no one.

In Finland, only recently people started staging their homes for sale, but nobody did it for rentals. So, I did. Landlords were notoriously known for being blood-sucking vultures. My mission became to create rental homes with heart and do land-lording with love. Doing it my way.

Solve Others Problems

To me, creating a home with a heart means designing it individually with a person in mind. Using color, textures, great materials and adding in some bold pizazz that renters cannot get anywhere else. A home the tenant loves and can be proud of. That sounds nice and all, but also expensive. It is. Especially as an income less stay-at-home mom.

One thing that working in Silicon Valley taught me, beyond being a pleasure to work with, was to always provide value. Companies today struggle with constantly needing to produce content. For social media and for marketing. I realized I could help them. I contacted a few brands asking if they needed photos and content. I shared my mission and since I had chosen brands whose values matched mine, that mission jived with them. That way, I solved a problem for them, content creation, and in return they gave me a sizable discount on their products. Solve a problem for others and it might solve yours.

Since I did not have billions of dollars for the renovations and staging, I did this: I learned how to do the renovations myself using high-end design ideas, just done creatively for less. I also created my own furniture through DIY Ikea hacks scouring the "for free" section on the local "Craig's List." I shared those projects, and fails (ahem, I mean learnings) along the way, on Instagram. But I was solving a problem other people had too—wanting new cool furniture, and home design for less. This ended up increasing my social media following, which made it more incentivizing for brands to collaborate with me. Solve a problem for others and it might solve yours.

Business Case Example

Here is a recent deal I made to give you an example of how it plays out in numbers. A 1970 one-bedroom apartment found on the Finnish version of the MLS. It had been there a while, and I was not sure why until I went to see it. It was listed as in "good shape" for $165k. It was in pretty poor shape, smelled like ass and had what looked like mold in the ceiling and bathroom (makes people freak out). I offered $150k. Offer

declined. A month later, it was still there. So, I offered $147k buying it
as-is with all the furniture (the realtor had shared the seller lived abroad,
so I saved him a trip). Offer accepted. Solve someone's problem and it
might solve yours. I sold most of the furniture online and made a few
hundred dollars. Some I saved and hacked into staging furniture.

The renovation estimate was $25-30k, everything needed to be redone.
The kitchen, the bathroom, all the surfaces. With that renovation cost,
the deal was a no-go. Which was another reason it had been for sale for
so long.

How can you make something like that work? Here's what I did instead
of a $10k full bathroom remodel: I cleaned it, fixed and painted the grout,
renewed the caulk (the mold was just surface due to poor ventilation),
cleaned the ventilation outlet, had a plumber update the surface pipes,
stencil-painted the floor tiles, added in a new IKEA vanity I found
online for $50 and DIY hacked, added in a new high-end sink I found
at a kitchen outlet, mirror, tap and glass shower wall. Thanks to a social
media brand collaboration, I got the stuff at a discounted price. Cost of
the bathroom renovation: $1,500. Increase in home value: approximately
$10,000. How is that for a return on investment?!?! Same thing with the
kitchen. Instead of a full re-haul, I pimped that bad boy. Painted the
cabinets and cabinet doors, added tile, updated the countertop, sink,
tap, handles and added in new appliances. Cost of kitchen renovation:
$2,000. Increase in home value: approximately $15,000.

Business Case in Numbers:

Purchase price: $147k

Renovation cost: $15k (including closing and holding costs)

Financing: 85% Conventional bank loan at 0.7% interest (I know, money is crazy cheap in Finland now).

Cash in the deal: $22k (I was able to use freed up equity from my previous BRRRR as additional security otherwise banks only lend up to 75%. Cash-out refinances are not offered in Finland as they are in the US). Plus, the $15k renovation (banks in Finland do not lend money for investment property renovations) = total cash in the deal **$37,000.**

After Repair Value (ARV): $190k

Equity Increase: $43k (ARV $190k-Purchase Price $147k)

Refinance: $43k * 75% (the maximum most banks in Finland refinance at) = **$32,250**

This means I almost got all my invested cash right back out and the rental income return becomes infinite. Remember, this was not my first, second or third deal. I have done a few of these that enabled me to put out that amount of cash.

I can hear you protesting with things like: "Easy for you to say, I have not worked at the world's leading communications agency," or "What if I do not have thousands of followers on Instagram," or "I do not live in a market that has crappy rentals." Sure, all valid points, but how far will that get you? What if you instead asked yourself these questions:

- What is everybody else doing and how can I be different?
- What do I know that can be of value to somebody else?
- What can I offer as a brand? Pictures, content? A collaboration?
- How can I use my creativity to add some pizazz?

- How can I do this renovation for $1,000 instead of $10,000?

Do YOU

And about the Tough Mudder race—guess what happened? I climbed the mountain, cursing the day I signed up, feeling beat being overtaken by so many. However, before I knew it, people started to fall out. They cramped up so badly that they had to quit before they had even reached the first obstacle. Meanwhile, my crawling ass steadily made it to the top.

Do not waste your energy comparing yourself to others. You are tougher than you think. Being you, and doing things your way, as scary and slow as it might feel, will take you further than you can imagine.

And PS. Don't wear a thong at a mountain marathon. One word: ass burn.

Maria Friström

In 2016, in search of balance, and financial freedom, Maria left a life of eating out, catwalks and a killer job in Silicon Valley for a life of Dickies and tool belts; DIY-rehabbing and renting apartments in Helsinki, Finland. And she loves it.

She started building her real estate portfolio from scratch as an income-less stay-at-home mom, and in a couple of years built a million-dollar portfolio.

In 2018, Maria founded a real estate investment company in Finland where she now works full-time as the CEO focusing on buy-and-hold rental apartments using the BRRRR strategy, while raising two toddlers.

She believes tenants have the right to live in a wonderful home they love, which is why she designs the apartments individually and creatively, adding some pizazz.

Maria is a public speaker and lecturer, podcast host and writer for the world's biggest real estate investing blog, Bigger Pockets. When she's not busy keeping her two toddlers from piercing each other with power tools, she loves meeting new people, teaching real estate and encouraging others to dare more.

She's been featured in The Finnish Landlord Association Magazine, Glorian Koti, Iltalehti, Helsingin Sanomat, Sijoitusovi, Duunitori, Finland's largest real estate investment podcast "Ostan Asuntoja."

Strength in Numbers
By Serena Norris

The strength of the team is each individual member. The strength of each member is the team.
–Phil Jackson

The year was 2011 when I sat at a computer desk in a small, closet-sized room with no windows, wearing a cocktail dress that definitely would not pass any school's fingertip test, jewelry that dripped off of me as if I had just robbed a department store, a face full of makeup and three-inch stilettos. Next to my office chair was a clothes rack full of men's silk-lined suits and specialty jackets with price tags upwards of $70,000 each. Above my head, surrounding me, were thousands of perfectly stacked perfume bottle boxes I imagined may topple onto me at any given moment. One step outside my office door was an opposite sight: marble floors, sweeping staircases, breath-taking displays made up of exotic-skin jackets, silk ties twisted to resemble mini sculptures and bouquets of color-coordinated flowers. Each day I was in the presence of top businessmen, political leaders, members of royal families from around the world and the occasional celebrity would stop by to capture a picture for their social media, since few could even afford the merchandise.

I was an in-house graphic designer for '*The most expensive store in the world*' on Rodeo Drive in Beverly Hills. My design work was featured in dozens of world magazines, on Santa Monica Boulevard billboards, on the designer's website, in the hands of Sheikhs to advertise our branded model of a Rolls-Royce Coupé—it seemed like a young graphic designer's dream. After all, that is what I went to college for and I had not even graduated yet. Within two months, I received a twenty percent raise and the CEO sat me down and said, "Tell me your life story. How did you get here? I want to know everything so I can hire more people like you."

At just twenty years old, what more could I have asked for at the beginning of what seemed like a promising career? But it felt like a prison. Besides my graphic design work, I had created new systems to revolutionize the inefficiencies in their day-to-day operations without recognition. I challenged leadership and their ancient ways of thinking to promote innovative ideas only to be reprimanded and belittled. I was objectified as a woman daily and often praised for how nice I looked more than my contribution to the company's success. After one too many days, or years, of wishing the San Andreas fault would shake and send a cascading waterfall of perfume bottles down to put me out of my misery, I quit and never looked back.

Besides my not fitting within the company's culture, I also longed for something so much *more* but at that time I had no idea what *more* was. During the same few years, I suffered sudden losses of two people who were very close to me and I felt a constant sense of urgency to take control of my life instead of waiting for life to happen. With a deep love for music, I got the wild idea to learn how to play guitar and get my friends (who coincidentally were amazing at playing the instruments that were needed) together to form a country music band. I had never performed on stage before, but I found someone to mentor us, hired a vocal coach, used my graphic design skills to build us a website and marketing campaign, walked into every bar we could find (underage) to sell our band to each manager and within six months we were playing gigs all over Los Angeles at least two times a month. We were good. I was good. It was the first time in my life I realized anything was possible if I believed that it was; that it was possible to create success out of nothing by aligning with a goal and putting all the right pieces together. It was also the first time, outside of playing sports, that I truly recognized the importance of being a part of a great team.

In 2014, I lived in Hawaii. As I was sitting in a laundry-mat waiting for my clothes to dry, I decided to read a certain book hoping to impress my then-boyfriend, who would not shut up about it. Little did I know it was the same book many first-time real estate investors read–and one of the only things that boyfriend would be good for. The book was *Rich Dad Poor Dad* by Robert Kiyosaki and Sharon Lechter. Like most, I was immediately inspired to do many things like creating a life by design with financial freedom, developing the skill of leveraging time for money and creating streams of passive income, but it also sparked a fire I did not realize had been lit within me my entire life.

At that moment, memories of my childhood started flooding back. Riding my bike around town to analyze all the houses listed for sale, grabbing their marketing flyers and going through open houses. I could not have been older than ten at the time. I remembered touring my father's and stepfather's remodels, since both were general contractors, and discussing floor plans with them often that I had created for fun, learning how housing systems worked and how to add value to a property. I had a passion and knack for something I did not realize I could apply in my life because I was blinded by the image of what I thought making an income should look like.

I manifested everything real estate, even before really learning the power of what that was. My clothes could not have dried soon enough before I moved back to my home state of Washington after living away for six years. Two days later, I met Tarl Yarber at my cousin's wedding, who later would become my mentor in real estate investing. We did not know we were about to walk into a new chapter in both of our lives. As he was leaving the venue, I told him boldly, "We're meeting for coffee next week!"

I jumped right in. I began working as Tarl's assistant and within the first year, we were managing up to twenty fix and flip properties at any given time. It was the beginning of Fixated Real Estate and we had zero systems. With just the two of us, our wheels were running like crazy figuring it out any way we could, leveraging real estate agents, contractors and absorbing every drop of knowledge they had to offer. Within five years, we built a core team of four badass people and successfully flipped (or BRRRR) just under a hundred single-family homes, but it was a long road to get there.

In the first half of our business, we were hungry and purchased any flip deal that made sense. We were consistently flipping the maximum number of properties our business could handle at a time while increasing the project scope and size of the projected profits. We were measuring the success of our business more by the production amount not realizing the impact it had on the overall health of our investments and ourselves. We were unknowingly challenging the old golden rule: *you can have it fast, good or cheap, but you can't have all three.* Hindsight is 20/20, but it was hard to recognize all of this at the time. It was not until 2017, when we reached the end of the year utterly defeated, drained, uninspired and unmotivated. We had spent the past two and half years grinding in the trenches, building up our systems and processes, adding people to our business to fill manpower needs and even though we were still making money, we were ultimately failing. We lost focus of why we pursued real estate investing in the first place—wait, why *did* we even get into real estate?! It was a miracle we had built such a strong core team without a clear vision. At that point, our team pledged to make a massive shift. We let go of our project manager who did not fit our team's culture, set limits on the number of projects we turned to eight to ten at a time, adjusted our buying criteria, changed team members' compensation structures, refined our processes and aligned our business goals to individual ones. We did what we should have done from the beginning: building real estate around our life instead of our life around real estate.

Throughout the journey of our business, I often struggled with what my best role within the team was and it took some time for our team to evolve into the structure it has today. One thing I knew for sure from the beginning was that my yearning was to manage and lead a team, but at 24, I was restricted by a lack of construction experience and leadership skills. Tarl and I worked well together from the start, but after I grew into a managerial role without a real understanding of what our personality and entrepreneurial types were, we struggled with unclear chains of command, ownership of our lanes and pinpointing our highest and best uses within the business. Also, I may have traded in the three-inch stilettos for boots, but as a young woman within a predominantly male industry, especially on job sites, there were occasional challenges of asserting authority. I often get asked how I have overcome the adversity of being a woman managing contractors and the simplest reply is, "It is all in the way you walk into the room." I do not let any ounce of doubt creep into my mind that the men will treat me any differently because I am a woman. If I allow those thoughts to manifest, then I will perceive their words and actions as so, and what I perceive and believe is the part that matters. I also learned there can actually be advantages to being the only woman on a jobsite.

I may have always had a desire to become a leader and drive a team forward but as I was gaining influence, I also had to learn the painful lesson of letting go. I will be the first to admit it, I can be a bit of a control freak. I was extremely independent at a young age and grew up with the mentality I could do everything better on my own. In school, whenever I had a group project, I immediately took charge, handed out small tasks to others and would keep the major responsibilities because I did not trust the rest of my group to do the task correctly. Today, I do the complete opposite. By creating simple team systems, communicating clear expectations of the results and the *whys* behind them, I quickly learned the power of delegation. It is safe to say we would not be where we are today without our business functioning as a team. So when and how did my need for control within a group change? It could have begun in my early twenties with my band in Los Angeles. It was a humbling experience relying on four other musicians, especially since they were much more talented than I was. Ultimately, my trust in my bandmates heavily contributed to both the band's success and mine.

Although important for a leader to understand themselves, identifying our team members' different personality types has been monumental in setting the team up for success. We utilize the DISC Personality Test. Specifically, Tarl typically aligns more with an *Artist,* someone who possesses extraordinary talent or skills that set them apart from others. An Artist lives for creating ideas and turning them into reality. I relate more to a *Manager-Leader,* someone who loves to manage people, create systems and processes, and monitor the operations of a business. By creating clear lanes between me, who aligns more with the manager role, and Tarl, the visionary, we have been able to mitigate internal management issues quicker as they arise. According to Tony Robbins, when these two types of personality types partner with each other, it increases the potential for a successful venture.

Besides the process of constructing our team by identifying our personality types and how they all fit together, the biggest hurdle for each of us individually was to apply what we learned from our assessments and identify the activities that would support our results: what would give us energy and what would drain our energy. Even though I have a natural desire to take charge and create and optimize systems, as I experienced even in my graphic design job, I often reverted back to focusing on activities that did not serve my highest and best use for my role, such as the actual creation of floor plans, design projects, etc. I may enjoy these activities because I am good at them, but I found that within business, they drain my energy instead of fueling my momentum. I now know that if I focus too much time on activities that are not my highest and best use, I will stop thriving. By identifying my own strengths and weaknesses and how to best apply myself, I have been able to combine a team's strengths together, unleashing a much higher potential for success.

When reflecting back, I went through periods of time minimizing myself to my surroundings because I believed my 'potential' would someday reveal itself. When in reality, it was there within me the entire time. I was busy striving to *become* something entirely different instead of simply embracing who I was, aligning myself with the right people and activities, developing a true understanding of myself and how to grow, and then ironing out the details. I would not have fully grown to understand myself in the way I do today without working with others as a team within our business. We can only go so far alone. By combining the right energies, it creates a stronger, synergistic outcome. By combining your strengths with others' strengths, you become a stronger force yourself.

Serena Norris

Serena Norris was born in Hawaii and raised in the Seattle area. Her passion for real estate started at a young age. With both her father and step-father owning general contractor businesses and her grandfather an architect, she was in and out of remodels from the time she could walk. When she was a child, she was often found drawing floor plans for fun, analyzing houses for sale in her neighborhood and discussing remodeling options with her father for his projects. After attending college in Los Angeles and working for a few years as an in-house graphic designer for a high-end fashion menswear company, she realized she had strayed away from her true passion and desire to build wealth in real estate. In 2015, Serena began her real estate career as an assistant to a house flipper and during the first year, the two were managing up to 20 projects at a time. Today, Serena is the operations/project manager, interior designer and in-house broker for the same company, Fixated Real Estate LLC, a small investment team that specializes in volume fix-and-flip and BRRRR single-family properties. By focusing on building strong, scalable and duplicable systems, the Fixated team has successfully "flipped" over $40,000,000 in single-family homes from Seattle to Portland. In 2017, Serena and the Fixated team created Fixated On Real Estate, a real estate community and monthly meetup that averages 150 investors, and the PNW Big Badass Real Estate Wealth Expo, a yearly 3-day conference that has brought 1,000 investors together and has raised $360,000 for charity in the past few years. Serena is licensed with Keller Williams Realty and a participating member in multiple young professionals and charity event groups in the Northwest. Serena has a work smart, play hard attitude and strives to lead their team by creating the systems it needs to flourish and to promote a healthy life-work balance. In her free time, she plays guitar, piano, various sports, and travels the world.

Working With Your Spouse
By Melanie Dupuis

Create the highest, grandest vision possible for your life,
because you become what you believe.
-Oprah Winfrey

"Ten multifamily properties before you turn 40… that is impossible!" is what the majority of co-workers, friends and colleagues would respond when I shared my 5-year goal with them. Sure, it seemed a bit aggressive, unrealistic and even unattainable at the time, but I had a passion for real estate and most importantly an immense drive for financial freedom. I wanted full control of my time and knew that I did not want to spend the rest of my life working 9 to 5. I also knew that I wanted more time with my kids and husband and wanted a flexible lifestyle to do what I wanted when I wanted. It was important for me to not only teach my three children to turn their dreams into a reality but prove to them that with passion, dedication and hard work, that anything is possible!

Getting Started

When I first met Dave, my husband and business partner, we both had a passion for real estate. I already owned two multi-family properties and he had a single-family dwelling. We were tired of living paycheck to paycheck and spinning our wheels in the rat race despite both having good, safe, unionized jobs with benefits and cushy pensions. We knew that to attain financial freedom as a couple, we would need to significantly expand our real estate portfolio, work as a team, stay committed to our goals and take massive action. There was no room, nor time for excuses. And so, we forged ahead *together*.

Contrary to what most people would have assumed, given the size of his shoulders and confident personality, Dave feared the unknown that came with real estate investing. Fear of the unknown kept him paralyzed from acting. "What about non-payment of rent, damage to the property, unforeseen repairs..." he would ask. I confidently replied, "We will figure it out together." Although I did not know all the answers, I knew that if we were solution driven instead of problem-focused, we would figure it out. Within the next few years, we purchased three multi-family residences together, but then we hit the most common financial roadblock - we ran out of money.

We had exhausted our savings, which left us without funds for the next deposit and we did not have the necessary equity in any of our buildings to fund the next deal. So, above working full-time, I started teaching part-time at our local college. Dave was on board and contributed by working additional overtime whenever he could. Being on the same page and equally putting time and effort eliminated any possibility of resentment down the road. Despite our drive and efforts, it was a slow, draining process and I quickly realized that working more wasn't the solution. At this pace, there was no way I would attain my goal of owning 10 properties before turning 40.

I often asked myself: "How are the millionaires doing it? How did they go from living paycheck to paycheck to creating true wealth?" After much thought, research and reflection, I finally figured it out. I was doing it all wrong. The key to success was to make money while I slept instead of trading my time for money while awake. This could all be done by leveraging debt. With this new reality in mind, I recognized that by wisely leveraging debt, I could finance deals through a variety of strategies, including the use of Other People's Money (OPM).

The possibilities became endless. I could buy properties through different strategies, including seller financing, retirement plans like RRSPs and 401Ks, promissory notes, etc. Now, with private funds, I was able to buy underperforming buildings which have rendered the biggest lifts and appreciation. Maximizing on each other's' complementary strengths to achieve explosive growth was a must! With Dave's outstanding ability to come up with endless creative ideas and strategies coupled with my ability to develop those into procedures and systems, we made creative financing possible.

12 in 12 Months

We needed to have a strategic plan to explode our growth. We did what we typically do and had numerous weekly couple/business meetings. These meetings are always extremely productive as we spend this time brainstorming and strategizing. These meetings have helped us expand our business and strengthen our relationship. We have discussed staff optimization, implementation of new systems, work-life balance strategies, goals and creating ways to involve our three children with real estate.

After numerous meetings, we were both committed to going all-in on this creative financing strategy and we crushed it! And that's when it happened - 12 multifamily properties in less than 12 months while using NONE OF OUR OWN MONEY! I must point out that we achieved this while still working full-time #sidehustle. These 56 units were purchased solely in our names. We achieved what most people told us we could not do, which was to attain tremendous growth while having sole ownership and no Joint Venture (JV) partner. We love this strategy as we get to keep 100% of the profit, equity and appreciation and can pass this wealth-building machine along to our children, which will provide generational wealth.

Growing that quickly meant we needed to ensure that we worked as a team and adjusted our priorities. For example, we both stopped watching our favorite TV shows and would get up very early to work on our business before the kids woke up. No time was spent micromanaging each other's tasks and second-guessing each other's work. Our focus was to collaboratively work on our massive goals by taking massive action. We strategically divided tasks/projects based on our skills and passion so our time would be spent wisely, and we ensured to respect each other's geniuses. Yet, we always made big decisions together. This includes whether to buy a certain property, terms/interest for private lenders, and when to refinance. Discussing these crucial decisions, along with our yin and yang personalities have been equally important for our growth and we used it to our advantage.

The Crash

Although we divide and conquer most tasks, we always attend conferences together. We use this time away from our kids as 'us' time, to do what we love and connect as a couple. One trip that was forever life changing. Less than two years ago, we were on our way to a real estate investing conference. It was a beautiful summer day and we were both excited to get on the road. So, we got up early, kissed the kids goodbye before they got on the school bus and were picked up by our shuttle. We were enjoying our time together, laughing, chatting and working on our laptops when out of nowhere, it happened and suddenly, we were in the middle of a horrific, life-threatening vehicle accident.

A careless transport driver swerving between vehicles hit a vehicle, who then hit us. Our Suburban instantly crashed into the guard rail and we flipped four times across the three-lane highway. I will never forget the horrific sound of metal against cement. It all seemed to happen in slow motion. Feeling completely helpless, I closed my eyes throughout it all and kept thinking to myself, "this can't be it" I must be there for my three young children. We finally landed on the other side of the highway facing oncoming traffic and upside down. Bloody, shaken up and in shock, we crawled through the broken windows and got to safety until the medics arrived. This traumatic and terrifying crash changed my life forever.

I was off from my full-time job with a severe concussion, which gave me plenty of time to reflect on my life, my dreams and how quickly all of it can be taken away. I thought about my three precious kids and how in an instant, because of a selfish, careless driver, they almost lost me... lost Dave. As weeks went by and after numerous visits with specialists, the symptoms slowly disappeared. The reality of going back to work was approaching and the thought of spending one more day of my life doing something I did not love made me feel physically ill. Perhaps it was the post-traumatic effect, but I just could not go back. Dave was 100% supportive and repeated what I had said years ago "We will figure it out together." Although my plan was never to leave my job at this point, I quit my job at only 39 years old. Though it was a bit terrifying, I must admit, being the youngest and only woman in that room to be able to pack my belongings and pursue my passion was the best decision I have ever made! Suddenly, I had FREEDOM!

Having an additional 40-hours a week gave me work-life balance. I can now see my little five-year-old son hop on the school bus in the morning and hop off the bus at night, attend every single school activity for my two girls, determine where I work when I work and best of all with whom I work with. The horrendous accident forced us both to realize our true purpose in life, which is helping others create financial, time and location freedom for themselves, through real estate investing. To foster this dream, we decided to write a book together and create a mentoring program that has helped investors across North America.

"Couple" of Tips

Working on building my real estate empire, with my best friend (Dave), is priceless. The best part about working with your spouse is working on your shared goals and your common inspiration - together. Just think about how much positive energy we are collaboratively creating!

Here are five critical tips that have helped us along the way:

1. Identify your "why" together. What is the true reason behind wanting to build a real estate portfolio? Hint: It cannot be just about the money.

2. Arguing is normal but be quick to get over it. Always remember the bigger picture, which is achieving your "why."

3. Be each other's sounding board. Spend time brainstorming ideas together.

4. Celebrate your successes! Whether it is your first property or your 20th, take the time to celebrate.

5. Communication! Do not assume your spouse knows how you are feeling and what you are thinking. Tell them and respect each other's feelings, ideas and opinions.

Being a young and determined female investor came with unwelcomed and uncalled for criticism by naysayers. Believing in myself, having a supportive spouse and remembering my 'why' kept me focused on my end results. People were quick to judge and to tell me my goal of owning 10 properties by the time I was 40 was impossible, unachievable and ridiculous. Looking back, I realize that although they thought I was being unrealistic, I was underestimating the strong, independent business woman that I am. I lacked confidence in my skills and had set my goals too low. I was capable of much, much more. By 40, I owned 24 buildings, over 100 units, quit my full-time job, had a bestselling book, became a speaker and mentor across North America, owned a property management company that won business of the year, won the 2020 Canadian Business Award as a Leading Expert in Real Estate Investing and achieved my three freedoms - financial, time and location.

I am not any luckier or more special than you are. I am, however, limitless and so are you. YOU are all limitless! YOU can achieve massive success if you truly believe that you can and then choose to take ACTION! So, ignore the naysayers, set massive goals, take massive action and achieve massive results. Join me, we are no longer the only woman in the room!

Melanie Dupuis

Melanie Dupuis, also known as Investor Mel, is an innovative real estate investor who, along with her husband Dave have SOLELY acquired over 100 apartments/24 properties in just a few short years. Using creative financing strategies, she has increased her portfolio significantly using none of her own money. With her husband, she impressively has 100% ownership of these properties, which means she keeps 100% of the equity, appreciation, and cash-flow!

Mel, the mother of three precious children, is proof that if you let nothing stop you, success can be yours. Following a life-changing highway crash in 2018, Mel and Dave wrote a Real Estate Investing book that achieved Amazon #1 Best Seller status very early into their launch. Her passion and determination to increase her portfolio at an impressive rate enabled her to quit her full-time job before turning 40.

With over 10 years' experience in real estate investing, property ownership and management, Mel understands the ins and outs of building a business and acquiring wealth through real estate. In 2019, she and her husband won the "Small Business of the Year" award, in North Bay, and they have also recently won the 2020 Canadian Business Award as Leading Experts in Real Estate Investing. She is dedicated to helping others create their own financial, time and geographical freedoms. She is a speaker and mentor throughout North America and has helped her mentees use creative and strategic financing to change their lives. Her online presence is impressive, with over 50,000 followers. You can find her on Instagram, Facebook, YouTube, LinkedIn and Twitter under her user name @investormeldave and on her website at *www.investormeldave.com. Ensure to watch her completely FREE Creative Financing Masterclass: (How We Bought 12 Properties in Less Than 12 Months) www.12in12months.com*

Riding the Silver Tsunami
By Leka V. Devatha

If you can't fly then run, if you can't run then walk, if you can't walk then crawl, but whatever you do you have to keep moving forward.
-Martin Luther King Jr.

The best thing that ever happened in my life was growing up in India. It was a life inundated with culture and strong family bonds. I lived with my parents, grandparents, uncles, aunts and siblings. I learned the most from my father, a life-long businessman and entrepreneur. His knowledge stems from his myriad personal experiences, trials and tribulations, and he would always emphasize two things to his children. His first lesson to us was always that family came first, no matter what, and that we were to take care of each other for eternity. His second lesson was to invest money wisely, and what was his favorite investment vehicle?

You guessed it: real estate.

I moved to Seattle at the ripe young age of twenty-four. I had just met and married the man of my dreams and this was where he lived. I had always felt I was destined to do something big, and that the ordinary life was not for me. So how could I tie my move to the land of freedom and opportunity to the fact that I was meant to do extraordinary things? I did not have the answer... just yet.

I had a dream job here as a merchandise planner for Nordstrom Corporate. I would have killed to have had this job throughout my career in India... anyone would. But over the next few years I spent climbing the corporate ladder at what was by all accounts a wonderful company with a fantastic culture, something did not sit right; I always felt like I was missing my true calling.

I casually investigated other career opportunities. During this phase of my life we built our primary residence, from the ground up, and I felt naturally involved in the design process. I thoroughly enjoyed it, and an idea developed... I could buy some land and build a home! Easy, right? Wrong.

I had no idea where to begin, how would I fund such a project? Where would I find the land? Was this even my true calling? I knew nothing about Seattle real estate, not the market, the industry, or how to start up a small business in the United States. And thus, began my hustle, slowly but surely. I learned to overcome obstacle after obstacle, grunting through every challenge that presented itself. I reached out and built my network and quickly discovered that I could do something far less risky than building new homes. Residential renovation demanded lower margins, shorter timelines, and had a smaller risk exposure than new construction. I had just stumbled upon something exciting!

We lived in a region with a thriving economy and one of the fastest-growing real estate markets, but with that came severe competition as well. Established flippers, international cash buyers and wealthy retail buyers all flooded the market. Convinced of the merits of building a wide network, I attended every meetup, whether on-line or in person. I would talk to anyone that would listen about how I was looking for my first deal. I joined a Mastery Program and watched every training video, built a long list of wholesalers and courted every private and hard money lender I could find.

A few months of dogged persistence eventually paid off with me landing my first flip in a popular suburb of Seattle. That project absolutely beat me up and the lessons I learned have stayed with me forever. Was it a struggle to find the right contractor? Yes. To stay on time and on budget? Yes. Struggle to sell? Yes, especially since I had listed the house for sale during Thanksgiving week. Did the inspection uncover issues? Yes! This had been far more challenging than anything I had ever done before, but surprisingly, I had enjoyed every minute of it. That was in 2014.

In the six years since I started my real estate investment firm, I have knocked out sixty-plus real estate transactions and renovated forty single-family homes. I joined a lending startup based out of San Francisco, as an advisor, and tested a new income stream as a realtor solely focused on investor clients. Through the years, I have stumbled upon a wide range of opportunities, but the most promising opportunities have often come from the hardest challenges.

One such challenge was a flip I purchased in 2018. It was a 3,400 square foot home in the city of Shoreline. The home had previously been used as an adult family home (AFH). When I bought it, I knew nothing about this, so I converted it to a single-family home, following my usual template. It had two entrances, each with its own driveway, and though it was zoned as a single-family, it had been used as a duplex. The home also had two kitchens and two living rooms. This project took an extraordinarily long time to remodel thanks to its sheer size and an overworked contractor who kept dropping the ball. We finally finished the remodel a year after purchase and listed it for sale in the spring of 2019. It was a popular time to sell homes, with days on market typically under two weeks. Despite all this, my home sat on the market for an entire month, forcing me to consider alternate exit strategies. The neighborhood this house was in is an extremely up-and-coming area of the county, so I knew that the house could make a fantastic buy-and-hold, if only I could find a way to break even on the monthly expenses. When in doubt, I have learned to always fall back on my large network, and on this occasion as well, they came through.

My stager first introduced me to the idea. She was an investor herself and said that house would be perfect for use as a renovated adult family home. I had never really explored or considered adult family homes up to that point, and what I discovered amazed me.

The Silver Tsunami

According to the U.S. Census, the Baby Boomer generation is the second largest in the United States, second only to Millennials. Longer life-spans – in part due to improving healthcare, and record low birth rates amongst young women, are both leading to what will be an explosion in the population that will reach senior age in the next decade. This phenomenon has been nicknamed the Silver Tsunami.

To put this in perspective, it is estimated that 10,000 people in the United States will turn 65 *every single day* over the next ten years. By 2035, the number of seniors living in the country will double from its current number to 41 million, and then double again over the following 15 years. The median age in the United States is expected to jump from 37 in 2010 to 41 in 2050. America is turning gray at an incredible pace and with that, so are the dependency ratio and the need for quality care facilities for seniors.

In 2010, 1.3 million people aged 65 and older lived in skilled nursing facilities. Since then, when the first of the baby boomers entered retirement, the average occupancy rate for both independent living facilities and assisted living facilities shot up from 63.6% in 2010 to 90.2% in 2015.

These trends are working together to create a gargantuan need for quality assisted care facilities in North America, of which adult family homes are one. Several aspects of renting out adult family homes make it an incredibly compelling focus opportunity for real estate investors. An adult family home, unlike much larger assisted-care facilities, typically houses six to ten senior residents and provides an individualized care service to its clients. It is managed by a resident licensed provider, with additional caregivers working in shifts to ensure 24/7 attention. The home is typically rented out to seniors on a per room basis with month-to-month contracts, although tenants certainly tend to be long-term, usually opting to spend the rest of their remaining lives in a single home.

Now, besides the obvious incentive of providing a much-needed service for the community, adult family homes can be an extremely lucrative business for real estate investors. Providers rarely have the means to buy and run their own adult family homes (nor is real estate usually their area of expertise), so the typical setup is for them to rent these homes from landlords. The rental term is considerably lengthier (five to ten years) than the typical single-family rental, often with the option to either renew the lease or buy the property outright at the end of the term. Leases are also usually double or triple net, and overall, net two to three times the monthly rent of a similarly equipped single-family home in the same neighborhood. In other words, a well-run adult family home in a suburban neighborhood of a city like Seattle could generate $6000 - $9000 in monthly rent, as opposed to the $3000 per house that a typical single-family home would generate in monthly rent, in the same neighborhood.

As you might guess, free money is a falsehood, and adult-family homes come with their own unique challenges. First, and perhaps rightfully so, the industry is heavily regulated. Licensing a property to run as an adult family home requires abiding by a whole host of state-specific regulations, since clients are often mentally or physically handicapped individuals needing special assistance. For example, ADA compliance requires single-story layouts, larger bedrooms, wider doors and hallways, ramps, and roll-in showers, just to name a few. Once these criteria have been met, the home needs to pass multiple inspections, a process that could stretch for months, depending on the state. Then the challenge comes to find a competent and state-licensed provider, getting the lease signed with favorable terms to all parties involved. Since the home is then used to run a business, the insurance, conventional loan terms, etc. are all also provided for only by entities that accommodate commercial properties.

After overcoming all these challenges, you will net a recession-proof, risk-free, long-term investment vehicle that offers both an amazing monthly cash-flow and considerable appreciation. Further, a few of these properties will dramatically alter a company's balance sheet and financial portfolio. The most important thing to remember in real estate is there is endless opportunity. I have met people that have had incredible success with everything from storage facilities to mobile home parks to drug rehab homes. Whatever your journey thus far, if you a) create a vast network, b) always adhere to a learner mindset, and c) have grit, you will have the successes you want, and achieve your dreams.

Leka V. Devatha

Leka moved to the US from India 13 years ago. Back in India, she had a successful career in fashion merchandising and when she moved to Seattle, she transitioned to Nordstrom Corporate. After working there for a few years, she realized that what she was really after was creating a legacy.

She quit her corporate job in 2014 and started Rehabit Homes, a company investing in Real Estate. Her first project took her 5 months to complete, and she made no money. The real takeaway, though, was her realization she had enjoyed every second of it. After a string of successful flips, she obtained her broker's license in 2017 and became one of the top-producing real estate agents in her office.

She has now flipped over 40 homes and has expanded her focus to include land development, acquiring long term rentals and building and running adult family homes. She also enjoys inspiring and motivating other entrepreneurs to build successful companies and, for this reason, hosts a meetup monthly to bring new and seasoned investors together. Occasionally, she still takes on massive renos!

Building a Business Through Social Responsibility
By Rachel Street

We make a living by what we get, but we make a life by what we give.
-Winston Churchill

It was a sweltering summer morning and I looked over at my dog, Johnny, who was panting beside me on the mattress on the floor, his nose bright pink from the heat. It was the type of oppressive heat that made you feel dizzy and burned your lungs when you breathed in, and I had not slept all night as a result. I was concerned that one or both of us would get heatstroke, so I put on Johnny's leash and got into the car where I drove to Wawa to buy a bottle of water and an ice cream to share. I parked under the Route 95 overpass and sat in the air-conditioned car for three hours and cried.

I had been living on the floor in a bedroom of a shell of a house I had bought, without a working kitchen, heat or air conditioning and I had been traveling to Planet Fitness to shower, since my bathroom barely dribbled out water. There was a roof leak in the back of the home that flooded the rear bedroom every time it rained, so my belongings were stacked in the front of the living room by the door, my clothes folded in piles on plastic I had put down to cover the dirty old carpet. None of my friends knew this, as I was ashamed of my situation and would let no one inside.

When I had bought the house, I had plans to make it my first investment property, and it was supposed to be the start of my new life after the recession (along with a health issue and subsequent botched surgery) derailed my opera career in Italy, where I had been living prior. I had rented the rooms in my primary home - a small row home in South Philly - and scrimped and saved for two years to be able to put a down payment on it, earning a very modest salary at my father's commercial mortgage brokerage. However, after I had gotten the investment property under contract, my father had unexpectedly fallen into a coma and the day after I closed on it, on Christmas Eve, he passed away. Suddenly, I was left without my father or a job. I knew that without a salary I could not pay two mortgages for long, much less be able to pay for renovations on the new house, and so I put my primary residence up for sale and moved into the shell.

The months that followed were a blur of grief and work, as I tried to finish out my father's business and provide for myself, and every night I came home to that depressing house, huddled around the electric space heater in the cold months and exhausted from the heat in the summer, embarrassed that I had gone from performing opera in Italy to living like this. Even though it did not feel like it, and I was almost certain that I would end up on the street, this move ended up being the best thing I ever did for myself, because it resulted in me starting both my real estate business and my construction company. I bought an old used Ford in North Philly for $500 and a bunch of used tools, and I worked as a realtor in the evenings, using my commissions to pay my bills and to renovate the house. I used my grief as fuel to work harder and longer, terrified that I would fail, and after about eight months, I had completed my first project.

The rest is history - countless successful construction jobs and flips, millions of dollars of real estate transactions, numerous awards and features in national publications and becoming the host of my own television show on the DIY Network - but there is one thing that never left me, and that is the feeling of living on the floor of that bedroom, teetering on the edge of financial ruin.

This career I chose has afforded me not only financial success, but more importantly it has allowed me to grow into myself as a woman, to claim my place in this world and provide an avenue for me to do something that I love and help people along the way. When I was struggling, finding support or help was next to impossible and I think sometimes people forget just how difficult and isolating struggles can be. As a woman in construction, at a time when I knew nothing, I was laughed at, hit on and heckled at construction supply houses. I was laughed out of the bank when I asked for a line of credit, I was taken advantage of by other contractors in whom I had put my trust and I didn't know anybody to turn to for help or advice. As I worked my way toward the other side of that, I wanted to make sure that my business contributed positively toward not just me but toward my community. In turn, I have received tremendous support from my community, which has boosted my business tenfold.

How I Implemented It - Doing Pro-Bono Construction Work

My story, aside from perhaps being a cautionary tale about choosing opera as a college major, is also a testament to how we are all just one life event away from throwing us into potential financial ruin. An unexpected illness, death or a sudden loss of a job, can send us catapulting out of our comfortable existence into true need very quickly. I was lucky enough to have a supportive family, a good education and a network of people I could turn to in order to at least point me in the right direction. But for many people, this is not the case.

Across the Philadelphia region, people struggle with illness, addiction, domestic abuse, advanced age or dealing with losing a family member. In real estate we have a unique portal into seeing just how deeply those issues can affect people. We come across women seeking a new place to live to escape abuse, we help sell the homes of those who cannot care for themselves any longer and we have all gone into homes literally falling around their occupants. In Philadelphia, we are experiencing a lot of development, but we still have a lot of our housing stock that is very old and in very poor condition. There are people living in buildings that are uninhabitable, without heat, without electricity or with water streaming in from their roofs.

I will never forget going into a dilapidated row home in North Philly, where the renter had jumped the electric meter and was using her electric stove to heat the house. The house was collapsing in the rear and one of her family members slept in the basement on a mattress covered in mold. The poor woman begged me to help her find a new place to live. These are unacceptable conditions for any human being to live in, let alone in a city where we also have so much wealth.

As I created beautiful spaces that contributed to an increase of value in the neighborhoods I worked in, I felt a responsibility to also help repair the homes of those in need, so we could help advance as a whole community instead of just widening the gap. Often, there are small home repairs, like a small roof leak, that can be easily fixed with a few hundred dollars or an hour or two of labor, but if left untreated, it can destroy a property. As I earned money from my jobs and flips, I set aside funds and extra materials to work on some of these projects. Ironically, as I became more successful and no longer so desperately needed it, suddenly everyone wanted to help me. People wanted to work for me, lenders wanted to give me money, suppliers provided me with free materials to use on the television show. I leveraged these relationships by getting materials and laborers donated to my pro bono projects in exchange for some free publicity for these companies. It was a win-win. I helped more people and those companies also benefited from the positive press.

Honesty and Integrity in My Work

Unfortunately, in the construction world, there are a lot of contractors who take advantage of their clients or do faulty work. When I started my company, I was usually the second or third contractor on the site and I made a business for myself by correcting the work of those who had come before me. Often, I felt so badly for some of these clients that I took jobs where I lost money or broke even, but unwittingly, this became a major source of advertising for me. After someone has been burned a few times by others and you fix their problem, you will earn a loyal client for life. Those clients referred me to their friends and family and hired me for bigger jobs down the line, this allowed me to find work easily by word of mouth only and make a name for myself as a contractor to trust. Now I focus more on doing my own flips instead of doing construction work for others, but even to this day, my projects are known for their quality of construction and attention to detail.

Respect for Everyone

One of my first clients was a young woman who told me she was getting estimates from several contractors after someone she hired had basically destroyed her house. She asked me a long list of questions she had prepared about the job and my company and I listened carefully and explained everything. I prepared a detailed estimate I went over with her a few days later and thanked her for the opportunity to give her a quote. I won the job and got many referrals from her. She later explained why she had chosen me. She said that the other (male) contractors that had come through before me had either been patronizing or tried to take advantage of her by quoting extremely high numbers. When she had tried to ask them questions, they either scoffed at her or told her not to worry her little head - that they would come in and take care of everything. She had chosen me because I had treated her with respect and made her feel comfortable. Likewise, I had done a job for an LGBTQ couple, who referred me to many others in their community for similar reasons, and as a result, I had created a niche for myself that became a fountain of future business.

Support for Other Women Businesses

One of the most shocking things, when I started as a contractor, was how little trust people place in women. As a woman contractor, one question I get on almost every job is "How did you learn how to do this?" I was constantly looked at with skepticism and, especially initially, I had to work extra hard to be taken seriously. While men, who were my employees, were trusted without question. I wanted to help create a path for other women in this career field, so I actively search out and choose to work with other women business owners wherever possible. In this way, I've created a community of trust and support. These days, there are a lot more women in the arena, and I am very lucky to call many of them friends. When my brand-new truck with all my tools was stolen, this community of women rallied around me and created a fundraiser to replace some of my belongings and get me back on my feet.

Bring Financial Education to Everyone

I used to run a free English as a Second Language (ESL) program for adults in South Philadelphia. I had started the program myself and as my students progressed, I taught other levels, eventually having over seventy-five students. This took up much of my time, but it was fun, and I made great friends along the way. (In fact, when I was redoing my first house, it was one of my students who came over to help me for free and teach me some new skills!) When I began selling real estate, my students wanted to learn more about my business, so I worked some real estate and financial education into the lessons. They were not only learning vocabulary, but about how to buy a home and start their own business. Several of my students invested in real estate and one of my students, a woman from Guatemala, who had never finished high school, even created a small portfolio of row homes in South Philly. I realized there were not a lot of resources for non-English speakers to learn about real estate, but there was great interest, so, since I speak Spanish, I advertised my services on Spanish-speaking Facebook groups. I created a network of Spanish-speaking mortgage professionals and inspectors and became known as a trusted resource in the Spanish-speaking community. This helped people in my community advance financially and helped me build my business.

Block Builds and Cleanups

One of the biggest complaints about contractors in Philadelphia is the noise and trash they bring to the neighborhoods they work in. Therefore, before I start a job, I give a letter to the neighboring houses to explain to them what I'm planning to do. I assure them I will try to keep noise to a minimum and only during reasonable hours and give them my direct contact information should they have any concerns. My crews also spend time at the end of each day picking up trash and sweeping the block, and we will often do small repairs for the neighbors at no charge. In exchange, those neighbors often become some of our biggest supporters and advocates, helping watch over our job sites or saving us parking spots.

Building Up the Next Generation

A few years ago, my scooter was stolen from in front of my house. A few months later, someone was caught riding it in North Philly. They were arrested and I was summoned to court. The perpetrator was a tall skinny 19-year-old kid, who was already in a detention center related to other minor charges. His father came to every court date and I felt bad that because of his age, he was going to have a charge on his record permanently over a juvenile mistake, which would really derail his life. I ended up working out a deal with his public defender, where he would come to work for me in construction for a few months, earn some money, learn some new skills and pay off the restitution. In exchange, the charge would be expunged from his record. A few weeks later, he showed up to his first day of work, a shy and quiet kid.

This experience really piqued my interest in working with teens, especially inner-city teens, and helping them to explore a career in the trades as an avenue to create a life for themselves. In Philadelphia, we have a high crime rate and many teens who cannot afford college, who have not received a proper education due to our poor city schools or who are aging out of the foster care system with no quality job prospects. This leads to a lot of teens creating a life for themselves by getting involved in illegal activities, often because they are not exposed to any other prospects. I began working with at-risk youth, giving talks about how to start your own business and how much money you can make in the trades, giving workshops to teach kids to use tools and hiring teens in the summers under my construction company.

College costs an average of $127,000 versus an average of $33,000 for trade school. Starting salaries are, on average $51,000 for a bachelor's degree versus $42,000 in the trades, but unemployment and underemployment are high for college graduates, whereas jobs in the trades are in high demand, and opportunities are only increasing. Plus, trade school takes an average of two years to complete, instead of the four years it takes to get a bachelor's degree (and 64% take longer to finish!) I love teaching kids about how to invest in themselves, become their own boss, and showing them what exponential profit looks like instead of becoming a slave to an hourly wage. Watching their eyes light up with the use of their first tool, seeing the fruits of their labor and watching them grasp the concepts of investment is really rewarding. I almost always get the question, "Miss Rachel, what is the first thing you bought when you sold your first property?" and my answer is always "More real estate." I like showing them how to invest back into themselves and they learn that they are worthy of investment.

It was also thanks to working with kids I met the most important person in my life. One of those kids who came to work for me one summer was a 16-year-old boy, who was a super hard worker, and we formed a very special bond. As the summer progressed, I knew what I had to do; I got certified to foster to adopt, and now I am honored to be able to call him my son.

Summary

Wherever there is great opportunity, there is also great responsibility, so as we contribute to building homes and raising values, we also must think about building up and contributing to our communities as well. And surprisingly, I have found that the more I have given, the more I have received in terms of clients, support, recognition and - most importantly - a support network of friends and allies.

Rachel Street

Rachel Street is a Realtor, Contractor, and Television Host. She is the Team Leader of the real estate team The Street Group at Space & Company and President of Hestia Construction, LLC, a woman-owned construction company offering full construction services and design-driven custom homes in her native Philadelphia. She is also the Host of *Philly Revival*, an HGTV and DIY Network TV show that follows her as she finds architecturally interesting properties that are run-down or abandoned, and transforms them into exciting modern spaces that also honor the history and unique original features of the home. Rachel, her construction projects, and real estate listings have been featured in many local and national publications, including *Philadelphia Magazine*, *The Philadelphia Inquirer*, *The Washington Post Magazine*, *House & Home*, *The Wall Street Journal*, *Parade Magazine*, *Curbed Philly*, *Forbes*, and *Insider*, among others.

Rachel and her company have been widely recognized for their social entrepreneurship and community service, which includes starting a program to provide free renovations and home repair for those in need, teaching English as a Second Language, mentoring youth and teaching them about the trades, and participating in neighborhood block builds and cleanups. She is also a Board Member for the East Passyunk

Business Improvement District. Previously, Rachel has previously worked in commercial finance as a Mortgage Analyst and Commercial Loan Originator, helping to underwrite and close over $300 million of commercial loans. Fluent in both Spanish and Italian, Rachel is also a classically trained singer, and has lived abroad in both Italy and Mexico. She has also completed extensive studies toward becoming a General Appraiser through The Appraisal Institute, and holds a B.S. in Vocal Performance and a Certificate in Construction Management from Temple University. Rachel has won numerous awards, including *Philadelphia Magazine*'s "Best of Philly 2019 - Best Contractor," The *Philadelphia Inquirer*'s "Influencers of Real Estate 2019- Rising Star Award," as well as awards for her community service and real estate sales volume.

Follow Rachel on Facebook at @rachelpstreet and Instagram @hestiaphilly

Hestia Construction, LLC: www.hestiaphilly.com @hestiaphilly

The Street Group: www.streetgroupphilly.com @thestreetgroup

Made in the USA
Middletown, DE
30 March 2021